WHAT WE CAN DO FOR EACH OTHER

D1374032

WHAT WE CAN DO FOR EACH OTHER

An Interdisciplinary Approach to Development Anthropology

Edited by Glynn Cochrane

B. R. Grüner Publishing Co., Amsterdam 1976

ACKNOWLEDGMENT

Thanks and acknowledgment are due several editors for permission to reproduce papers, and portions of papers, that they had published: *Oceania*, for the land tenure piece; *Finance and Development*, for the piece on the World Bank; *Economic Development and Cultural Change*, for the piece on the relationship between the micro view of the anthropologist and the macro view of the economist. E.D.C.C. is published by the University of Chicago Press.

Copyright © 1976 by Glynn Cochrane.
Printed in The Netherlands.
ISBN 90 6032 069 7

For the student who cannot ask for a reference

CONTENTS

Preface   ix

Contributors   x

Introduction   1

I.   *Paul Streeten*
        Why Interdisciplinary Studies?   5

II.   *Scarlett Epstein*
        The Ideal Marriage Between the Economist's Macro Approach
        and the Anthropologist's Micro-Approach   10

III.   *G. B. Masefield*
        Anthropology and Agricultural Extension Work   29

IV.   *J. Duncan M. Derrett*
        The Roles of Anthropology and Law in Development   43

V.   *Glynn Cochrane*
        The Importance of Legal and Anthropological Training   58

VI.   *C. Douglas Rider*
        Teacher Training for the Alaskan Bush   67

VII.   *Glynn Cochrane*
        Anthropology at the World Bank   75

Conclusions   83

PREFACE

The Third World badly needs the kinds of expertise that only anthropologists possess. What special attributes does anthropology have? What would be the utility of an anthropological dimension in development work? My own experience suggests some obvious strengths: first, anthropological methods of data collection are capable of producing unique information of high quality; second, anthropologists have an interest in human motivation which is of inestimable value in making calculations about development policies and their consequences; third, anthropologists have a humanistic orientation which usually causes them to examine the ethical and moral basis for change against the needs of the people whose wants those changes are supposed to serve. These pieces show what an interdisciplinary approach to development anthropology looks like, what it can do, and what kinds of training are required. This book will serve its purpose if it helps stimulate, among serious students of the discipline, the kind of discussion and debate that are a necessary prerequisite to change in the way universities train their anthropology students, and the kinds of jobs that graduates are helped to acquire, and encouraged to take.

Some of the contributors are not anthropologists because I felt it important, in a work that aspires to be interdisciplinary, to have views and perspectives from outside as well as inside the discipline of anthropology.

Amsterdam
September 1975

The Contributors:

Paul Streeten is Warden of Queen Elizabeth House and a Fellow of Balliol College, Oxford University

Scarlett Epstein is a Professorial Fellow at the Institute for Development Studies at Sussex University in Brighton, England

G. B. Masefield is Lecturer in Agricultural Science at the University of Oxford

J. Duncan M. Derrett is Professor of Oriental Laws at the School of Oriental and African Studies in the University of London

Glynn Cochrane is Professor of Anthropology and Public Administration at the Maxwell Graduate School of Syracuse University

C. Douglas Rider is an educational anthropologist who has recently worked in Alaska

INTRODUCTION

It seems odd to have to begin by saying that in one sense this book is not about anthropology at all since the concern expressed is really with relations between anthropology and other things. With respect to the discipline itself, what is now said can be thought of as a sociology of knowledge that is based on the cognitive behavior of anthropologists. The interdisciplinary approach to anthropological training that this work examines can provide more jobs for graduates in anthropology, can more effectively bring anthropological methods and techniques to bear on world problems, and can result in more effective attainment of traditional academic concerns. Why do we need to become more interdisciplinary and service-oriented?

An interdisciplinarian is someone capable of using the theories, methods, and techniques of two or more of the disciplines that constitute the social and/or natural sciences. Advocacy of a genuine and feasible interdisciplinary approach does not, of course, imply that one person can know everything. It does, however, imply that an anthropologist recognize the same problems that are commonly accepted by the other disciplines; that the anthropologist know enough about other disciplines and professions to be able to estimate which will, on a particular occasion, supply the intellectual bricks, which the empirical mortar, in the effort to achieve progress. In a general sense, the interdisciplinarian has in-depth expertise and knowledge in one field and acquaintanceship with the capacities of other fields. What this implies for the anthropologist is the importance of realizing that interdisciplinary approaches have an intellectual and a human dimension. One cannot flourish without the other.

An interdisciplinary nonacademic anthropologist has to be the kind of human being who can, on occasion, offer to play a quite minor role while economists or nutritionists take the limelight. An interdisciplinary anthropologist may not be able to work on his or her favorite kind of problem in his or her favorite area. Interdisciplinary anthropology needs human qualities not all students of anthropology will have or even want to have.

After all, anthropology too is learned behavior, and anthropologists have human wants that must be gratified. Some anthropologists like the security that comes from being the only person who knows the kinship behavior of a remote people; others like teamwork and working with other people. Some anthropologists develop strong emotional ties with the areas where they have studied; others become attracted to particular theories or methods and will work anywhere that provides an opportunity to show the appropriateness of their point of view.

Anthropology is a series of tools and methods whose use does not necessarily recommend the appropriateness of one political or theoretical ideology rather than another. Commonality among anthropologists rests on their methods and theories rather than on the broad goals such individuals seek as representatives of many cultures, religions, and political persuasions. There are, of course, differences between, say, Tanzanian anthropology and Chinese anthropology, or between British anthropology and Russian anthropology. This difference relates to the *ends* of these different kinds of anthropology rather than the *means* employed by the various kinds of professional anthropologists to reach those ends.

When, for example, one bears in mind the fundamentally political nature of development, it is surely not surprising that the anthropology of a conservative and a liberal must obviously differ with respect to what they want to analyze and the kinds of measures they would support or recommend. The choice of problems is quite a human matter — in much the same way that a person decides to become a historian rather than a psychologist.

What can anthropologists do that other disciplines and professionals cannot do? What can anthropology not do? These questions need to be more fully explored than is the case at present in most schools of anthropology. It's all very well, for example, to understand the importance of values and beliefs as a reason for why a health program has failed. But how do you make the program successful?

The complaint now heard is that anthropologists are not adequately prepared for careers in development work. Senior officials of most large organizations, whose work needs anthropology, say that anthropologists are people with few bureaucratic skills. Demographers interested in population work in poor countries generally think that sociologists have better quantitative skills than social anthropologists. Anthropologists are not generally believed to be knowledgable about mass communication techniques; rural development specialists say that anthropologists have inadequate statistics for output per hectare or acre, factor proportions, probable effects of agrochemical augmentation policies, credit mechanisms, etc. Nutrition experts often want to know about the content and food value of various traditional foods and the possibilities for effective vitamin-additive or protein-fortified food programs. However, there is little training for anthropological students in this field. While one can generally think of one or two very useful anthropological studies in these areas, the coverage is by no means global, since at the time when the data were collected, fieldworkers had not thought — or been requested — to ask such questions.

Anthropology's early reputation rested to a large extent on the fact that the anthropologist was usually the only person in contact with traditional peoples who would publish that experience. Much of the knowledge collected during fieldwork had appeal because of its curiosity value. But that situation has changed, and what passes for anthropology now is often a matter of common knowledge or almost common knowledge among many other social scientists and those who have lived among or near the particular people being written about. When translated into everyday language, anthropology is often not terribly intellectual or difficult to understand. It wasn't meant to be. But most anthropology has been, and continues to be, produced for other anthropologists. This has important consequences.

The absence of an organizational base is a very heavy handicap in developing an interdisciplinary focus. Potential employers have little influence in the training of anthropologists. Few academic anthropologists have had any period of service with an organization which would help them to give students the results of their own personal experience. Public administration, sociology, psychology, and development economics have had their university curricula or programs shaped by a knowledge of the requirements of service in governments and agencies. Political scientists, sociologists, economists, and psychologists all have undertaken long stints in various government organizations.

The discipline is too shot through with individualism. Anthropologists are not usually trained to solve problems considered important by other social and natural scientists. Anthropology is perhaps the most individualistic of the social sciences, and anthropologists with their strange clothes, habits, and customs often seem to strive to express their own individual uniqueness. Research is individually conceived, individually carried out, and individually written up. But anthropologists need to be prepared for teamwork with other social scientists. Someone trained entirely in anthropology might be forgiven for not being able to sympathize with the reasons for the existence of political science, public administration, or social psychology. But then each of the social sciences has a series of ideological roots.

An interdisciplinary approach must succeed on quite pragmatic grounds rather than as an article of faith. The basic intellectual justification for an interdisciplinary approach is that it produces insights which are more useful than those available within a single discipline. Nor should an interdisciplinary approach be allowed to become a mechanism for preserving the individuality and intellectual isolation of the anthropologist. Through adoption of an interdisciplinary posture the anthropologist cannot continue the idea that he or she alone can do everything. This would run against the need to encourage teamwork. It would run against the fact that one person cannot know everything.

The training of anthropologists, if it is to be interdisciplinary, must be more oriented to the concerns, special techniques, and methods of other social and natural science disciplines. Anthropology alone is not a suitable form of training for interdisciplinary work. I believe that if one is to be an economic anthropologist, then one must have training as if one were going to become an economist. Similarly legal, psychological, or agricultural training. But creating a profession has other implications.

I have frequently heard among anthropologists the complaint that economists, because of their facility with numbers, have made off with all the good development jobs, while anthropologists, whose opinions and insights are felt by the anthropologists themselves to be more realistic, though usually qualitative, are seldom even listened to. Though the complaint seems to have an element of 'sour grapes' to it, there is the point that it illuminates a condition that is perhaps more commonly thought of in relation to anthropology than the other social sciences. Different economists will be able, independently, to arrive at the conclusion that there will be roughly similar rates of return on an economic investment project. But will several anthropologists give the same advice, if consulted, about a particular investment project? I suspect that most potential users of anthropology think the answer is 'no', intuitively sensing that the cherished individualism of the anthropologist is at variance with the degree of uniformity of judgment and predictability that characterize the objectivity and verifiability of professional statements. Anthropology needs to convince potential users of the discipline that it can be a profession whose members can be relied on to perform with the degree of uniformity and reliability associated with engineers, doctors, and lawyers.

Paul Streeten distinguishes between three distinct meanings of interdisciplinary work, which are often confusing. These three meanings have radically different implications for the method of work adopted and therefore for the conclusions. According to the first meaning, it is the special training in their conventional disciplines which makes the members of a team useful for the purposes of solving a practical problem. According to the other two meanings, the methods of the conventional disciplines have to be either extended or more or less radically revised in order to do justice to the reality studied. Interaction between variables in developing societies are often different from those in developed societies and the raison d'être for existing frontiers between disciplines is therefore often absent. On the other hand, ignoring or transending frontiers in studying one type of society often yields a bonus for the study of industrial societies.

WHY INTERDISCIPLINARY STUDIES ?

Paul Streeten

_____

Given the importance granted to the views of economists these days, a status
conscious anthropologist might sometimes complain that he is being used only
to provide fodder for the canons of the economist. A self-respecting anthropologist might refuse to have all the important questions asked by the economist
and to be reduced to a handmaiden, supplying low-class empirical material for
the high-class analytical structure of another discipline. Questions of status and
precedence are, of course, not of concern to serious scholars; on the contrary.
John Maynard Keynes looked forward to the day when economists would have
become like mechanics, when they 'could get themselves thought of as humble,
competent people, on a level of dentists ... .' (Keynes, 1933).

There are three quite distinct reasons for interdisciplinary, multidisciplinary
or supradisciplinary work. Each has different methodological implications.
First, a practical problem (improving nutrition, locating an airport, controlling
population growth, planning a town) may call for the application of several
disciplines. In the cooperative effort the disciplines are not transcendend but
brought together to solve a particular set of practical problems. The prevalence
of planning at all levels has contributed to the cooperation between different
disciplines. The planner has to draw on all relevant knowledge and skills. This
practical need to bring all relevant methods, data and information to bear on
the solution of a specific problem does not affect the methods used in the con-
tributing disciplines. On the contrary, it is just because they are specialists in
their fields that the different members of the team have a contribution to make
to an integrated solution. We might think of them as members of a Royal Commission investigating problems of conserving our environment or deciding upon
the location of a new airport or planning a new town.

Second, it may be the case that certain assumptions, concepts or methods,
hitherto applied only to one sphere of activity, yield illuminating results when
applied to another, previously analysed in quite different ways. There has
been some invasion of economic concepts and methods into the territory of
political scientists and sociologists. Thus, the assumption of maximizing behaviour has been fruitful in analysing the behaviour of consumers, firms and
farms. Its success has encouraged its application to political activities such as
voting and party formation. Calculations of economic returns have been ex-

tended from profit-making investments to education, health, birth control and the allocation of leisure time. Occasionally, though much less frequently, concepts used in political theory have been applied to economic problems. Albert Hirschman's use of 'voice' as an alternative to 'exit' is an interesting example (Hirschman, 1970).

Third, it may turn out that for a particular time or region the justification for having a separate discipline does not hold. This justification for a discipline consists in the empirical fact that between the variables encompassed by this discipline and those treated by another there are few interaction and the effects of any existing interaction are weak and damped. Only then are we justified in analysing causal sequences in one field, without always and fully taking into account those in others. We may all agree that society is a system and that all social variables are related, but with growing differentiation of functions and standards, some relationships are stronger than others. This justifies us in separating, say, business responses from family responses, or economics from anthropology.

If interdependence between variables normally studied separately is strong, or, though weak, if reaction coefficients are large, or though small, if they change size for moves above a critical level, there is a case for a merger of disciplines. This is sometimes called transforming parameters into dependent variables. Family ties and economic calculus, land tenure and responses to incentives, religious beliefs and commercial motivation may in this way interact. Where interdependence of this kind occurs and where the interdependent variables belong to different disciplines, there is a case for interdisciplinary work.

It is possible to draw two quite different conclusions from such interaction. First, it might be said that what is called for are not interdisciplinary studies but a new discipline that constructs concepts and builds models appropriate to the conditions of underdeveloped societies. In this case, we should have to discard concepts like employment, unemployment, underemployment, income, savings, investment and construct altogether new terms.

Second and less radically, the existing concepts and models may continue to be used, but their content may have to be changed or their definition modified.

The difference can be illustrated with the concepts 'capital' and 'investment'. Conventionally, 'investment' is defined as the addition of physical pieces of equipment, plant or stocks in order to raise the future flow of products or services above what it otherwise would have been. 'Capital' is the stock of these items that has resulted from past flows minus depreciation through use and obsolescence.

Now it is possible to enlarge this concept so as to cover all forms of expenditure that lead to a larger flow of future output, not only those that result in physical items of machinery, constructions or inventories. This would include 'investment in human capital', such as education, health and, at low levels, nutrition; possibly expenditure on birth control if we are concerned with raising income per head; expenditure on institution building and shaping attitudes. All this can, in principle, be covered by an enlarged concept of 'capital' and 'investment', as long as one condition is fulfilled: there must be a fairly systematic connection between the devotion of current resources (that might otherwise be used for current consumption) and the resulting flow of extra output. These resources need not be the only condition for the enlarged flow of output, but they must be systematically linked to this output by a fixed technical coefficient or at least by a range that is not too wide.

But if the link between current resources and extra output is only tenuous, so that a given result can be achieved with widely varying inputs, or the same inputs can lead to widely varying results, or if the results can be achieved without devoting any current inputs, or, in spite of large current inputs, no results ensue, the notions of 'capital' and 'investment' become inapplicable and we have to focus on those factors on which the outcome truly depends. The output of a factory may be within wide limits a function of the degree of capacity utilisation which, in turn, will depend upon the quality of the management; the result of a family planning programme may be only tenuously linked to the money spent on clinics, doctors, nurses and contraceptives but largely depend upon economic, social, cultural and religious attitudes of couples. The quality of the administration, the system of land tenure, the solidarity between different classes, the ethnic origin of the entrepreneurs, the history of the country may be more important determinants than the amount of resources. If this is so, no new wine can be poured into old bottles; the bottles themselves have to be changed.

In either case, we may in the process of analysing social phenomena in underdeveloped countries incidentally gain new insights into those in advanced industrial countries. Studies of the caste system may illuminate trade union behaviour and demarcation (jurisdiction) disputes; Scrutiny of the capital/output ratio may change our view of the production function; a wider concept of capital may throw new light on our own problems of industrial management. If this happens, it will be a bonus over and above what we had bargained for.

How then does anthropology fit into all this? In the first case for interdisciplinary work - the team approach - anthropologists will be used for their traditional training. If a land reform or a birth control programme or a tourist project is proposed, they will be able to point to 'constraints' in the beliefs and mores of the people, or they will be able to point to beliefs or institutions which can be mobilised and on which the proposed reforms or projects can be built. Nothing new or radical is required here.

The second case is more interesting. I suspect that economic method could illuminate some anthropological work and probably the other way too. While I know of some crossdisciplinary work of this kind between economics and political science, I do not know of any between economics and anthropology.

The most interesting possibilities are opened up by the third case, whether in its reformist or radical version. It is quite clear, for example, that an agricultural production function in many underdeveloped countries should count among its inputs, not only land, labour, fertilizers, water and power, but also levels of education of the farmers, nutritional standards, distance from town, health, systems of land tenure and of family kinship. All these variables are likely, in some societies, to be systematically related to agricultural production.

But it may turn out that the whole notion of a production function is wrong or misleading. Perhaps there is no systematic relationship between inputs, whether of fertilized land (physical capital) or of educated farmers (human capital). It may be that output depends upon variables that have been constructed and analysed by anthropologists: the relationship between majority and minority groups; religious beliefs (the Protestant ethic); or kinship systems. Or again, at a different level of discourse, it may be that large increases in output beyond a decent minimum are not a crucial component of development either at this stage or ever. The society may have opted for an alternative style of development, in which the ever-growing production of material goods is rejected. It prefers containment of wants and aspirations to growing production to satisfy evergrowing wants and infinite aspirations. Or, through a shift in valuations, unemployment may be converted into leisure. If this is the case, the crucial questions will have to be asked by the anthropologist or the sociologist. He has to construct the concepts and it may be that it is then the economists' turn to fill the boxes constructed by the anthropologists. Which of these possibilities should be realised will depend, partly, upon empirical conditions, but, ultimately, upon our valuations and our choice of a style of life.

Hirschman, Albert O. (1970). *Exit, voice and loyalty.* Harvard.

Keynes, John Maynard (1933). 'Economic possibilities for our grandchildren', reprinted in *Essays in persuasion.* London: Macmillan.

Is economic anthropology simply a situation in which an anthropologist works on economic matters? Does such an anthropologist need a background in economics? Scarlett Epstein sees a positive role for suitably trained anthropologists collaborating with economists in development work designed to meet the needs of very poor people. Having received anthropological and economic training Epstein is qualified to make clear the value of an interdisciplinary approach and the fact that acquisition of such education requires perseverance on the part of individual students.

THE IDEAL MARRIAGE BETWEEN THE ECONOMIST'S MACRO-APPROACH AND THE SOCIAL ANTHROPOLOGISTS' MICRO-APPROACH *

T. Scarlett Epstein

Introduction

Interdisciplinary studies are rapidly becoming the vogue in tackling Third World economic problems. I for one welcome this development. In fact I can claim to be a representative specimen of interdisciplinary economics.

I was fortunate enough to be trained first in economics by Ely Devons and Arthur Lewis, and subsequently in social anthropology by Max Gluckman and M. N. Srinivas, all outstanding men in their respective fields. The problem this interdisciplinary training presented to me is well exemplified in Arthur Lewis' response to the first report I submitted in 1954 at the outset of my fieldwork in South India. I gave an ambitious list of the various kinds of economic data I planned to collect as well as an outline of sociological factors I wanted to investigate. He strongly advised me to leave all the 'sociological nonsense' to the anthropologists and to concentrate on the serious business of collecting economic data. In this instance it was fortunate that I did not follow my supervisor's advice. I am convinced that without the examination of sociopolitical variables in the villages I studied I would have been unable to understand the process of rural economic development, and my analysis would have lacked insight and become largely sterile. By 1962, when my report was published, Arthur Lewis had come to appreciate the importance of 'interdisciplinary' economics, for the generously agreed to write the foreword to my book (1962).[1]

My academic training in fact qualifies me equally as an 'anthropological

*) This paper is the revised version of an earlier draft presented to the Continuing Symposium on Interdisciplinary Economics, Indiana University. I gratefully acknowledge Professor H.K. Schneider's invitation to participate in this Symposium, as well as his permission to publish my contribution in this form. I also want to thank Professors G. Dalton and J. Rosen for their constructive criticism, which I found most helpful in re-writing this paper. Needless to say, I accept full responsibility for the shortcomings that still remain in it.
1) W.A. Lewis, 'Foreword', in: T. Scarlett Epstein, *Economic Development and Social Change in South India* (Manchester: Manchester University Press, 1962).

economist' (ie. an economist conversant with sociological approaches), as well as an 'economic anthropologist', (ie. an anthropologist familiar with economic concepts). The latter breed of social scientists, though still regrettably small in number, is rapidly growing. Unfortunately, the former is yet a very rare animal indeed.

I am not merely suggesting for frivolous reasons the analogy of 'marriage' in discussing the union between the economist's macro- and the social anthropologist's micro-approach. Though it may have its amusing aspects, it is fundamentally a serious comparison.

To begin with, there does not yet seem to be any clear consensus on what type of marriage this is to be. Is it supposed to be a 'love marriage' where both partners approach the union with equal enthusiasm and are prepared to merge their individual interests and 'husband-wife' roles become interchangeable? Or is it to be a 'marriage of convenience', where each partner retains his separate identity and interacts with the other in clearly defined spheres only and where roles are strictly differentiated? Or again, is it to be an 'arranged marriage' where the elders decide that a union is desirable and the young couple concerned have no choice but to accept their judgement, yet resent it?

In applying the analogy of 'marriage' to interdisciplinary economics I think we can rule out the arranged type from the start; a 'love marriage', though highly desirable, is likely only in micro studies when one and the same individual has been trained in more than one social science. For the relationship between macro- and micro-studies we are left with a 'marriage of conveniece' which, if approached in the right spirit by economics and social anthropology, should and can result in an excellent working relationship. With this in mind I begin by examining the 'courtship' between the two disciplines, and continue by discussing specific examples of the advantages to be derived from the interdisciplinary framework.

Courtship.

Raymond Firth points out that the beginnings of the study of economic anthropology can be traced far back in the nineteenth, and even into the eighteenth, century. He lists a number of our illustrious ancestors (1967:2). Karl Marx and Max Weber certainly also rank as proponents of interdisciplinary studies: Marx probably qualifies as an economic anthropologist for, he concentrated on examining the effect of economic factors on social organization, whereas Weber seemed more concerned with analysing the impact of sociological variables on economic organization and therefore can more readily be included under the category of sociological economist. Most of these early exponents of interdisciplinary economics propagated the science of 'political economy'; under that umbrella it was regarded as respectable for economists to concern themselves with other than Western societies and to consider other than purely economic variables.

Marshall, the father of modern economics, made the break with that tradition. He summarily disposed of the economics of 'savage' societies in the well-quoted passage in which he talks of the irrational and custom-bound behaviour of savages (1936:723).

In Marshall's defence it must be said that when he wrote his epoch-making *Principles of Economics* in 1890 only few anthropological studies were available, and most of them were devoted to some of the more esoteric aspects of 'savage' societies. However, he set the pattern for the subsequent advance of economics. He carved out for study a particular field of human activities, (ie. concerned with price and wage formation) and subjected it to deductive reasoning. This process of delineathing the field of one discipline has resulted in research with blinkers. In covering the same problem one social science often does not know and does not even want to know what the other is doing. We have to thank Adam Smith for pointing out the advantages of specialization. However, overspecialization can be just as inefficient as lack of specialization altogether. A realisation of this is becoming apparent not only in the social but also in the natural sciences.

Significantly, among modern social scientists the anthropologists were the first to try and break out of their disciplinary straightjackets. The methodology of social anthropology easily accounts for this phenomenon. Social anthropologists almost always study microcosms and are concerned with a *system* where the interaction of the different social variables becomes glaringly obvious. Admittedly, few anthropological studies deal specifically with economic phenomena. However, many modern anthropological reports do include a great deal of economic data, even if these are generally only a by-product of the study of the study of social relations.

Herskovits' *The Economic Life of Primitive Peoples* (1940) represents, to my mind at least, the first open approach by social anthropology to modern economics. In this pioneering work we can find numerous passages, for instance, 'The principle of maximising satisfactions by the conscious exercise of choice between scarce means is valid because we find that this does occur in all societies' (1940:24) which indicate a ready acceptance of some of the basic economic pronciples. However, anthropology had, at the same time, serious reservations about the general relevance of economics. Herskovits critically examined the applicability of modern economics to primitive societies. His eclectic appraisal of economics emerges from statements such as, 'The *generalised* nature of the mechanisms and institutions that mark the economies of all the non-literate, non-machine societies, explains the difficulties that arise when we attempt to apply the more refined concepts of economics to these societies, or when we attempt to test some of the more debated hypotheses of economic theory by reference to them (1960:11).

Economics fiercely rebuffed these early advances made by social anthropology. Economists insisted on keeping their lily-white virginity, and feared being soiled by contact with *real* people and their behaviour. Knight's now classic review of Herskovits' book clearly illustrates this attitude. He said that 'the relationship between observation, induction from observations, and inference 'a priori' principles forms the very point of the problem of collaboration between the social sciences. . .' The principles of economy are known intuitively; it is not possible to discriminate the economic character of behaviour by sense observation; and the anthropologist, sociologist, or historian seeking to discover or validate economic laws by inductive investigation has embarked on a wild goose chase' (1960: 512). Knight scornfully criticised Herskovits for his emotional bias which corrupts scientific study and exposition, (1960:514). In spite of this contemptuous rejection of anthropology by economics, the 'young maiden' economics did not turn down altogether her 'anthropology suitor'. Knight did concede that it would be highly desirable on general grounds for economists to know more about the facts of economies other than their own' though he grudgingly continued: 'even if no direct use is made of it'. He then added a further indignity in saying that 'authentic facts are not necessarily more useful than travellers' tales based on superficial and largely false impressions — the bane of modern anthropological science — or even outright fiction or poetry!' (1960:517).

Anthropology did not accept lying down this severe rebuff. Herskovits in his rejoinder categorically declared that he disagreed entirely with Knight's statement that 'economics, in the usual meaning, as a science of principles, is not primarily, a descriptive science in the empirical sense at all if by this is meant that principles are to be divorced from facts' (1960:526).

Thus happened the first open confrontation between the young suitor 'anthropology' and the young maiden 'economics'. If the rapprochement had by now been succesfully completed and the account had no more than historic interest I need not have mentioned it here at all. Alas, these very same issues still hamper the successful cooperation between anthropology and economics. Admittedly 'economic man' has become an unfasionable topic; its axioms are no longer recorded in a connected and explicit way in any recent economic textbook. Yet the model is still fundamental to economics; remove the assumption and much of the superstructure of analysis would collapse.

Though no modern economist would hold that all the human characteristic referred in the Model apply generally without qualification, no-one has as yet worked out what qualification should be applied where or attempted to weight its importance. The insistent retention of the economic man assumptions and the isolation from reality in economic studies has made the wooing anthropology question the wisdom of the pursuit. A number of anthropologists concerned specifically with studying economic relationships came to the conclusion that economic theory has little, if anything, to offer in analysing primitive societies.

For instance, Sahlins remarked implicitly that the question is whether economic choices are specifically determined by the relative values of the *goods* involved. In primitive societies where price fixing markets are absent and social relations channel the movement of goods, the economy is organized by these relations (1960:391). Undoubtedly it is easier to study those forms of behaviour which are readily measured in terms of money, but this is a matter of expediency rather than principle. The problem of choice is not limited to exchange economies. All human activities involve the expenditure of time, which is a universally scarce resource. Salisbury's use of time as a measuring rod is a brilliant exposition of the successful application of modern economic concepts to nonmonetary economies (1962). Anthropologists find themselves increasingly working in societies where the economy is at least partially monetised and where it is relatively easy to establish market prices for subsistence activities. This probably accounts for the increasing number of researchers who follow Firth's pioneering work (eg. 1929) in the field of economic anthropology. The wooing by anthropology of economics has thus continued, in spite of the fact that economics played hard to get.

A Marriage of Convenience?

The courtship between social anthropology and economics clearly indicates that the former made all the advances, though often too with serious reservations, while the latter declined to get involved in any more formalised relationship. As long as economists solely, or mainly, concerned themselves with industrialised — and largely depersonalised — economies, they did not feel the necessity of consulting their fellow social scientists in solving their problems. Economic man seemed to represent industrial societies reasonably well. This allowed economists like Knight, to indulge in deductive reasoning without being in danger of being too far removed from the realm of reality.

The economists' isolationism, however, was radically affected by the fairly recent but rapidly growing concern with development problems. The increasing political importance since the last war of the Third World and the glaringly obvious gulf between levels of living there and in the advanced industrialised societies is responsible for this shift in emphasis in economic studies. Immediately after the last war, when more and more previously dependent countries became independent nations, the new creed of development economists began to preach that maximisation of the rate of economic growth in Third World countries, measured in terms of gross national product, would, within a reasonable span of time, greatly reduce, if not eliminate, the disparities between industrialised and developing economies. This simplistic belief was the immediate outcome of deductive reasoning based on the economic man model.

It did not take very long before the error of this oversimplified judgement became obvious. 'During the 1960's it has become recognized that formulation of economic objectives purely in terms of economic growth is not sufficient. The first development decade of the UN is now recognized as a failure despite the fact that the developing countries met the overall income growth objective of 5% per annum. It failed in what what was the originally unstated, but more and more generally recognized, corollary objective of translating the gains from growth into rising standards of living for people and primarily for the poorest' (ILO; 1972:59). This honest and perceptive statement made by ILO is reminiscent of the tale of the sorcerer's apprentice: many development economists, based their analyses and plans on the economic man model found appropriate to industrialised societies and they barged in where angels feared to tread. They did not realise that their own doings were helping to exaggerate the Third World's socio-political problems they in fact aimed to eliminate, namely, unemployment and poverty. Now that they have called forth the 'magic broom' of maximising growth rates, they find it extremely difficult to suggest means by which it can be got back into a more amenable framework. This has made it apparent that deductive reasoning based on the economic man model cannot provide the right formula for ensuring a more equal distribution of income either between different parts of the world or within any one country.

McNamara, in a recent address to the Board of Governors of the World Bank, made the rather obvious statement that 'increases in the national income — as essential as they are — will not benefit the poor unless they reach the poor' (1972:9). Though a truism, it is only slowly being recognized by the rank and file of development economists. McNamara stressed in his speech the political implications of a growing maldistribution of income between different parts of the world and particularly within developing countries themselves. 'It is only a question of time before a decisive choice must be made between the political cost of reform and the political risk of rebellion . . . Social justice is not only a moral imperative. It is a political imperative as well' (1972:17). With these statements McNamara seemed to suggest a resurrection of 'political economy' — economic studies with a broader horizon — and he is by no means the only advocate of such a reorientation in economic studies. However, among many economists Robbins' definition of their subject appears still to be generally accepted. Accordingly, they do not regard choice of ends as part of their concern. This is another reflection of their blind faith in being able to separate economic from all other social variables. Yet can any perceptive individual realistically claim that in the development process means and ends can be effectively kept apart? In fact those economists who advocate maximising the overall rate of economic growth and concentrate on means while ignoring ends, helped to reentrench a powerful elite. As a result this elite has developed vested interests which now exert considerable influence over the formulation of policy aims and provide a serious obstacle to any attempt at restructing the distribution of income. Economists therefore indirectly effected ends as well as means.

McNamara advised Third World governments to shift public expenditure towards those who need it the most by initiating surveys on the effects of their current patterns of disbursement: 'Where do the funds really go and who benefits most (1972: 17). He went as far as to offer the Bank's financial support for such surveys. Development economists are thus not only encouraged but also forced to face reality — the thing Knight tried so desperately to avoid. There is a growing realization among many leading development economists of their own discipline's inadequacies. Why is it that the Third World has defeated so many economists while advanced societies still lend themselves fairly readily to economic analysis. What is the major difference between advanced and less developed societies which has baffled economists?

In contrast to industrialised societies in LCDs the majority of people often 80 to 90% — lives in highly localised rural communities. Within these small-scale societies inter-personal relations tend to be multiplex to a far greater degree than they do in developed countries. The small range of social links is reflected in a greater density of relations between a limited number of rural dwellers: economic relations linking the same individuals as master and servant as well as creditor and debtor, are frequently parallel and reinforced, for instance, by kinship ties, political patronage, and ritual relations. The same individuals face each other in a number of different roles, and the set of norms applicable to any one role therefore tends to spill over into other relationships. It is this multi-dimensional linkage between different economic, political and general social variables within the large number of rural microcosms in the Third World, which constitues the major stumbling-block to the economist and his retention of the 'economic man' model macro-approach.*

Studies at grass root level have been, and still are by and large, the domain of social anthropology. Its methodology highlights the micro-approach by taking a small universe as the object of study and examining it in its totality. Very rarely, if ever, is the universe randomly selected. This lack of statistically representatives sampling has made many social anthropologists reluctant to suggest testable hypotheses on the basis of their findings; they talk of 'their' peoples and frequently regard them as unique: for instance they say 'the Bonga-Bonga do this' or 'the Kukukuku do that'. Such statements, though they may be important in negative terms — in disputing general assumptions about behaviour — have no real positive value. Economists label them as 'woolly' and stress the necessity of numerical predictions. Quantification has in fact become the deity worshipped by many economists who maintain that social scientists conducting micro-studies in LDCs must be forced out of their verbalising shells into the computer room. Only there can they jointly test and develop their views in a framework useful to planners (Lipton, 1968:15).

Quantification is certainly a much neater way of analysis and provides a clearer basis for predictions, but is it the only means by which testable hypotheses can be

*) The significance of these multiple relations is discussed in greater detail by M. Moore, (1974:99)

advanced? Social anthropologists, though they are increasingly involved in quantifying their enquiries, often feel at a loss to put numerical values on what are inherently and basically non-quantifiable variables, such as extended family ties, prestige, religious and ritual relations. To quantify these would often introduce an unjustifiably arbitrary judgement into social anthropological studies.

In view of this it is important that economists should come to acknowledge that qualitative analysis is a necessary part of any developmental study; moreover, that qualitative hypotheses can also be subjected to rigorous tests. To prove my point here I refer to my own research in South India. In 1954-56 I studied the impact of regional irrigation on the socio-economic system of two Mysore villages. In the concluding paragraphs of my book I argued that economic development, which I defined as an increase in per capita output, need not necessarily produce economic change. Only where the new organisational system was incompatible with features of traditional economic organization did I discover a change in economic roles and relations. But wherever there was such economic change I also found corresponding changes in political and ritual roles and relations as well as in the principles of social organization. For the societies I had studied I established a positive correlation between economic, political, ritual, and organizational change, with economic change being the determining variable. I concluded that 'the possible general validity of these functional relations has to be tested by many more studies of economic development and social change' (1962:332)   Though I had arrived at these hypotheses by way of detailed numerical enquiries, in themselves they postulated qualitative rather than quantitative relationships. Yet the hypotheses have been put to the test and verified by comparative research conducted in rural Sri Lanka by German social scientists, as well as by my own return in 1970 to the same Mysore villages I had studied 15 years previously. Wangala, the wet village, continued to resist involvement in the wider policy, and is still much more tradition-bound than Dalena, the dry but economically diversified village, where inhabitants have much wider political horizons and where social change has been comparatively radical.

The theoretical implications of these functional relations between different types of economic development on the one hand and socio-political changes on the other are obvious. I do not need to enlarge on them. Obvious also, to my mind at least, are the practical lessons for planners. Yet I have found no evidence that plans for economic development in India or elsewhere have in fact incorporated these lessons. This has induced me to plead for greater concern with regional development. Irrigation is of vital importance in many parts of the Third World where rainfall is often too little and/or too irregular ro allow farmers to realise anywhere near the full potential of their land. Thus irrigation schemes are bound to play an important part in rural development. It would be wasteful if wet land farmers had to divert their attention from culticating to provide for themselves the additional services they require. Every irrigation scheme will, at least at the margins, touch on land that cannot be irrigated. The comparative disadvantages of dry land farming in an irrigated region makes alternative income opportunities more attractive to these villagers. It is thus important that planners utilise and foster the competitive drive of villagers for the benefit of the region as a whole: special loans and training facilities may be provided for small-scale entrepreneurs from such dry land villages. This could help to facilitate and speed up the integration of irrigated and dry land villages into a regional economy' (1973:235).

This is but one of many examples which clearly indicates not only the desirability but also the sheer necessity of complementing microresearch by macroanalysis in development problems. There is a whole big area of research in Third World development which seems to provide the ideal basis for a successful 'marriage' between the different social science disciplines. Here there is a field where interests overlap and where each partner to the 'marriage' should consider it of mutual benefit.

The Successful Marriage: Economic Anthropology and Anthropological Economics

I trust that this lengthly preamble which outlined the preconditions for a 'marriage' between economics and anthropology has set the stage to mount a more detailed examination of individual case studies. In what follows I am focussing on two problems I have encountered in different field situations. Each of them, on the face of it, appears to fall within the strict and narrow boundaries of economics: rural wages in South India and sale of cocoa by indigenous New Guinea growers. In the presentation and analysis of these two case studies I am endeavouring to highlight the insight that can be gained from a joint application of economics and social anthropology to development problems.

Rural Wages in South India

My return to the same Mysore villages I had studied 15 years earlier provided me with the comparatively rare opportunity to reexamine, quantitatively as well as qualitatively, the same socio-economic variables. This study of the same microcosms at two different points in time enables me to show conclusively that the rich have become richer while the poor became poorer, not only relatively but also in absolute terms. I have detailed evidence to show that while total village income increased considerably due to the further extension of irrigation accompanied by a period of soaring sugar cane prices, the gulf between rich and poor villagers has also widened. Moreover, by concentrating on these microcosms I am able to analyse the process of increasing impoverishment of the poor — the very problem McNamara advised Third World governments to investigate. Admittedly, my microcosmos do not represent a statistically valid sample, and therefore my findings do not readily lend themselves to wider generalisation. Yet I submit that the hypotheses resulting should be worthy of testing and the practical suggestions emerging should at least be investigated on a macrobasis.

Before setting out the hypotheses and their practical implications, a brief outline is necessary of the intra-village socioeconomic mechanisms which help to resist external attempts in improving the economic level of the poorest villagers and raise their social status. These attempts are in line with India's officially expressed aims of a casteless, egalitarian welfare society, which so obviously failed in the villages I studied. Why? The answer to this question reflects the complex relationship between different economic and social variables.

The few wealthy became considerably richer not only because of economic phenomena, such as their ownership of increasingly large areas of irrigated land which yielded them sufficient surplus to benefit from the soaring sugarcane prices and enable them to invest in cane crushers, but also because they managed to prevent the break-up of their joint families, continued their hereditary labour relations with resident functionary and Schduled caste households while at the same time employing the more productive migrant workers on a purely casual basis, and because they managed to reaffirm their economic dominance by securing positions of political power and insuring appropriate ritual status. Similarly, there were inter-connected reasons for the increased impoverishment of the poorest, The village Scheduled caste households, have become poorer not only because real daily wage rates by 1970 were reduced to 60 per cent of their 1955 levels — simply because wage rises lagged behind price rises in this period of rapid inflation — and the competition from migrant labour reduced the number of days work they now find, but also because discrimination on the basis of caste put them at a disadvantage in competition with members of the regionally dominant caste for the still scarce employment opportunities in the nearby growing town. The rapid rate of population growth in India, where men/ land ratios are already high, results in increasing numbers of landless migrant labourers. The increased supply of labour by far outstrips demand and therefore depresses rates of cash wages. This helps the larger farmers to ride on the tide of inflation while the landless labourers are almost swallowed by it.

Legislation relating to minimum agricultural wages has remained completely ineffective in South India and the purchasing power of daily cash wages declined. Yet at the same time the customary system of fixed annual rewards, where it continues to exist, remains unaffected. I have argued elsewhere that a prescribed hereditary system of rights and duties is a mark of a stagnant economy and offers a minimum of security to villagers living in an environment over which they had little control: bad seasons provided a minimum of subsistence to all villagers while good seasons facilitated economic differentiation between those who controlled agricultural output and those who merely carried out the menial tasks (1967:250).

The involvement in the wider market economy of previously largely isolated and predominantly stagnant subsistence economies has resulted in a change of emphasis away from average productivity in bad years to marginal productivity under growth conditions. The traditional village motto of 'live and let live' is being replaced by 'change and economic betterment'. In Dalena, the dry land village with a diversifying economy, many bought irrigated land in neighbouring villages and extended their economic relations over a wider area beyond the borders of their home base. Accordingly they severed their hereditary relationships with local Scheduled caste households and altogether ceased to give annual rewards. In Wangala these relationships still continue and the quantity of annual rewards in kind has remained unchanged. In both villages cash wages in real terms have fallen. There has been no attempt on behalf of the wealthier Wangala farmers to exploit their dominant position *vis-a-vis* their dependent households so as to reduce the quantity of annual rewards in kind distributed at harvest time.

This difference regarding labour relations between Dalena and Wangala as well as the apparent inconsistency in Wangala farmers' behaviour can be readily explained if we accept that the same individuals can be motivated by different considerations for different activities involving the relationship between the same individuals. The dominant incentive for most farmers is to grow sufficient food to keep first of all their own families and secondly their dependents alive. Dalena's dry land can no more produce anywhere near enough food for its resident population. This fact forces villagers to seek support from outside their home base and is responsible for landowning farmers shedding the responsibilities for their Scheduled caste dependents. Wangala is still a more fortunate village: lands are sufficient not only to grow enough of the staple food crops of paddy and and millets, but also to produce a substantial surplus of cash crops in the form of sugarcane. Wangala farmers indicate profit-maximising tendencies when concerned with cultivating sugarcane: they are subsistence oriented when concerned with growing their own food crops. Several economic and social factors are responsible for Wangala farmers being prepared to continue paying traditional fixed annual rewards in kind: they want to ensure at least a basic supply of resident labour; they depend on Scheduled caste households for the performance of essential life-cycle rituals and there are other social as well as emotional bonds linking farming masters with their dependents. Yet when it comes to cultivating cash crops and paying cash wages farmers aim at maximising returns. They never consider cash wages in terms of purchasing power equivalence; all they are concerned with is the labourers' performance. Rural labourers on the other hand have practically no bargaining power, *vis-a-vis* their employers. Supply of labour far exceeds its demand. Individual labourers thus have no choice but to accept almost any pay and conditions of work they are offered. Wangala resident Scheduled caste households accept their lowly social status and the caste discrimination practised against them in return for the minimum subsistence local farmers provide for them. They do resent the fact that employers prefer migrant labour, but they see no possibility of forcing their request for more work within the village, or finding employment elsewhere.

On the basis of my study of rural wages in the context of Mysore villages I postulate the following hypothesis: net population growth in rural communities with a skewed income distribution accompanied by, or following the introduction of, cash crops and consequent monetisation will in a period of inflation result in cash wages falling in real terms; whereas the quantity of customary rewards in kind remains unchanged. This analysis has obvious practical implications: it suggests the possibility of tying basic agricultural wages to an equivalent in kind. If rural rewards are to keep up with rising food prices it would seem sounder to try and introduce agricultural minimum wages expressed in terms of a fixed quantity of the staple crop grown in the different areas. It should be easier to get farmers to revert to a barter economy, to which most of them are well accustomed at least in Mysore, and which involves multi-role relationships by persuading them to pay in kind, rather than legislate for a minimum cash wage which is likely to have to be continuously raised as prices go up.

I suspect that economists and planners will regard this suggestion as a retrogressive step and therefore reject it. 'But the expression of wages in kind, the tying of the reward for labour to a tangible quantum of food, does not mean a general reversion to barter even in the wages field, and in any case, if this is retrogression, can the constant deepening of the already desperate poverty of so many millions of men, women and children be called a progression (Spate; 1973:XV)'. Here it should be stressed that the introduction of wages tied to rewards in kind as an isolated measure on its own cannot suffice to ameliorate the plight of India's landless labourers. Rather a 'package of palliative measures' is required in this context. Briefly they consist in planning regionally integrated economies where landowners pay progressive land taxes and landless labourers are given priority in employment outside agriculture, while applied research helps to increase the productivity of small holdings and rural wage rates are tied to rewards in kind.[1] It is now left to macro-economists to examine the wider generalizations and ramifications of my micro-findings.

[1] A more detailed discussion of these palliative measures can be found in my *South India: Yesterday, Today and Tomorrow* (1962:243)

Sale of Cocoa by Indigenous New Guinea Growers

The Tolai of the Gazelle Peninsula of New Britain are generally regarded as the politically most sophisticated and economically most advanced people of the whole of the Territory of Papua and New Guinea. When the Australian authorities started a crash agricultural extension programme immediately after the war to make up for their previous neglect, Tolai farmers were encouraged to plant cocoa, a crop well suited to their environment. In order to prevent the haphazard planting of cocoa trees through bush areas and to facilitate disease control, an ordinance was introduced in 1952 to regulate the growing of cocoa; each grower is required to register his cocoa trees. The Melanesian big-man system provided fertile ground for economic development and the Tolai rapidly planted larger and larger areas with cocoa. Unless steps were taken to organise the native industry so that it had efficient processing and marketing procedures, there was a danger that it might become chaotic. Concomitant with the growing cocoa industry among the Tolai was the development of their native local government councils. This led to the establishment of the Tolai Cocoa Project (TCP) ownership of which was vested in the Tolai local government councils. With a Bank loan guaranteed by the authorities it established a number of fermentaries throughout the Gazelle Peninsula. The TCP was a non-profit making institution. Each Tolai grower who wished to have his wet cocoa beans processed and sold by the TCP, registered with one of the fermentaries, which paid cash on delivery, kept a record of quantities involved and paid a final settlement after the consignment had been sold and operating costs deducted. In spite of its obvious advantages to Tolai cocoa growers and the pride they took in it, the project began to face serious competition from European and Chinese traders soon after its inception. The drift away took on increasing proportions. As Tolai cocoa production increased so increased the proportion sold to independent traders.

The Australian administration became increasingly more concerned with this drift away from the project primarily because of its financial implications. Expert economists were called to examine the problem. True to their kind they explained the drift-away simply in terms of prices: in 1960 for instance the project offered a down payment of 6d. per pound following by another 2d. as a final settlement. Chinese traders paid once and for all 7d. per pound of wet beans. Economists argued that though this involved a loss of 1d. per pound sold to Chinese traders, quite apart from frequent short weighing, growers preferred the larger immediate cash payment to the greater return the TCP insured in the long run. This might have been a plausible explanation had Tolai been short of cash at the time. However, they were extremely thrifty and most of them had considerable cash savings. Thus even when the TCP increased the cash downpayment to the price paid by Chinese traders the drift-away continued.

Subsequently, the Administration turned to management consultants for advice. These experts examined the operations of the TCP and diagnosed the trouble as a structural one: they suggested to convert it from a public utility into a limited company with a profit incentive. This change was resented by the Tolai themselves at the time and therefore was not implemented. In any case, even the Administration doubted its efficacy. What then may have been the deciding factor for this increasing proportion of indigenously produced cocoa being sold outside the project? This question has puzzled many of the people concerned. Some regarded cocoa sales to Chinese traders as a sign of plain irrationality. The most outspoken critics of 'irresponsible' attitudes were some leading Tolai who themselves were often guilty of selling their cocoa outside the project. While support for the TCP was shown openly and sales records kept by fermentories, sales to independent traders were always conducted secretly.

My field work from 1958-60 in Repitok, a Tolai parish helped me to throw light on this subject (1968:126). Among other things I investigated were the people's kinship system, pattern of inheritance, landholding and residence, as well as inputs, outputs and sales of cocoa. My study enabled me to discover what seems a feasible explanation for the Tolai cocoa growers' irrational sales pattern.

The Tolai are by tradition a matrilineal people with a predominance of patri-virilocal residence. In other words, a man belonged to the kingroup of his mother's brother and had rights to garden land vested in his matrilineage. However, he usually settled on marriage near his father's residence. Unless his mother's brother also lived locally and controlled land there, he had no rightful claim to land near his father's place. As long as land was ample and food gardening involved shifting cultivation this presented no problem. In fact there was a customary obligation on the part of the father's matrilineage to provide gardening land for their sons. This used to be one way whereby matrilineage elders managed to keep their claims to certain land tracts alive and remembered. Rapid population growth accompanied by extensive plantings of perennial crash crops resulted in increasing demands and competition for land. Sons could no longer be so readily accommodated in their father's parish, unless they had claims to land there on the basis of their own descent group. Still the practice of patrivirilocal settlement continued. This led to an increasing proportion of land being cultivated by men squatting on lands of their father's matrilineage. Many a Tolai father wanted to ensure that at least part of the money earned from cocoa, which his son had helped to plant, would go to the latter's credit. Yet according to the customary inheritance pattern a man's sister's son rather than his own son had first claim to inherent his property, crops, money, and all. In order to circumvent the tarditional pattern of inheritance and give their own sons a better start in life, many Tolai tried to avoid having records of their property and earnings: they planted part of their matrilineage land with cocoa without registering the trees and sold the wet beans clandestinely to Chinese traders, who, unlike the TCP, kept no records of payments. This enabled their sons to accumulate the proceeds from cocoa sales without leaving any evidence of the amounts involved. On the old man's death his own matrilineal kin would thus not be able to claim the money as theirs.

Their were many conscientious and shrewd Tolai who were keen to ensure the project's success and disliked the idea of selling their cocoa to independent traders for less money than the project paid. But they were caught in a dilemma and could not see a way out. The conflicting pulls, emanating from their customary inherit ance pattern on the one hand and from their attachment to their own sons on the other, account for the apparently irrational and irresponsible behaviour of many dignified and respected Tolai men.

On the basis of this analysis I postulated in 1968 that unless the project abolished growers' sales records the drift away from the project would continue. Shortly afterwards the project was re-organised and sales records done away with. This worked almost like magic and reduced the proportions of Tolai grown cocoa sold to independent traders.

There are a great many peoples living in LDC's who, like the Tolai, are by trad- ition matrilineal and settle patri-virilocally. The analysis of New Guinea cocoa sales thus might have application elsewhere. It is left to the macro-economist to apply these micro-findings to a wider framework.

Conclusion

The analysis of the two problems I outlined clearly indicates the advantages to be derived from interdisciplinary studies. Both problems were basically economic ones. However, a narrow economic approach in their analysis would not have been fruitful; in the case of the New Guinea cocoa sales subsequent happenings have shown the futility of the single discipline approach. I must take it clear here that I am not advocating that interdisciplinary micro-studies suggest an immediate panacea for all development problems. All I am claiming is that interdisciplinary studies may help our understanding of certain development phenomena where single disciplines fail to do so. 'The fulfilment of human potential requires much that cannot be specified in purely economic terms' (Seers, 1959:5).

Interdisciplinary studies are becoming increasingly important in the analysis of development problems. It has become a commonplace that macro-plans with- out micro-knowledge just do not get implemented *and are therefore bad plans* (Lipton, 1968:14). Yet no one has as yet been able to define with any clarity what is involved in interdisciplinary studies. Most economists still only pay lip service to the idea. Some social scientists consider that the interdisciplinary ap- proach requires the complete breaking down of all barriers existing between seperate disciplines. If this were so it would involve the restructuring of the total field of social science training and research. Although desirable, I fear that this is a long term project whereas we are facing serious development problems right now. These cannot wait the long term process of social science re-organization. By way of compromise I offer two separate yet interdependent suggestions.

(1) *Inter-disciplinary Micro-studies*

Students concerned with development studies at micro-level should be required to train in at least two social science disciplines. I am thus advocating a full merger of separate disciplines within one and the same individual. Past performance in the field of development studies indicates that the only really interdisciplinary research has been conducted by individuals who are interdisciplinary social scientists in themselves, such as economic anthropologists, anthropological economists, political sociologists, etc. The alternative is multidisciplinary micro-research, whereby a team of social scientists representing a number of different disciplines approaches the same phenomenon from different angles. Such research does not seem to work as successfully as the individual interdisciplinary study.

(2) *Macro- and Micro-studies*

I am afraid I have been unable to discover any signs of such a 'marriage of convenience' already in existence. Yet an increasing number of social scientists and politicians profess their support for such a union. If so many of the people concerned want it, whu has it not yet taken place? The major obstacles seem to be timing, quantifying and planning. Macro-economists, and in particular, planners, usually turn to micro-studies when encountering a problem which does not lend itself readily to analysis within the narrow boundaries of economics. They expect micro-research not only to have the answers readily available but also in quantifiable form. They do not seem to appreciate that good micro-studies involve a lengthy spell of field work. Serious micro-researchers refuse to be bulldozed into producing quick results. This difficulty of timing and quantifying is responsible for much of the antagonism and mutual resentment existing between macro-economists and social anthropologists. The gap separating the two complementary approaches to development problems can be reasonably easily bridged, though:

Macro-economists should be in a position to plan years ahead their needs for micro-data: for instance, what types of problem in what areas microinformation will be required. Such plans would provide interdisciplinary micro studies with an overall framework. Needless to say I am not advocating restricting all micro-studies to fit into this macro-pattern. However, such a scheme would

enable macro-economists to subject micro-findings to large scale statistical enquiries, whereever possible, as well as incorporate the qualitative micro-data in
macro-analyses.

Under such conditions I anticipate a fertile marriage between the macro-
and micro-approach to development studies. Its offspring should ultimately
be a new model of the SOCIO-ECONOMIC MAN to replace the outmoded
'rational economic man'. Such a new model would provide the basis not
only for more realistic economic analysis but also for more theoretical de-
duction in anthropological studies of LDCs. If this were to materialize it
would ensure that macro- and micro-research would live together happily
ever after!

Bibliography

Epstein, T. Scarlett (1962), *Economic Development and Social Change in South
India*. Manchester: Manchester University Press.

Epstein, T. Scarlett (1967), Productive Efficiency and Customary Systems of
Rewards in Rural South India. In: Firth, R. (ed.), *Themes in Economic Anthropology*. London: Tavistock Publications.

Epstein, T. Scarlett (1968), *Capitalism, Primitive and Modern — Some Aspects
of Tolai Economic Growth*. Canberra: ANU Press.

Epstein, T. Scarlett (1973), *South India: Yesterday, Today and Tomorrow —
Mysore Villages Revisited*. London: MacMillan.

Firth, Raymond (1929), *Primitive Economics of the New Zealand Maori*. London:
Routledge & Kegan Paul.

Firth, Raymond (1967), Themes in Economic Anthropology. In: Firth, R.(ed.),
Themes in Economic Anthropology. London: Tavistock Publications.

Herskovits, Melville, J. (1940), *The Economic Life of Primitive Peoples*.
New York: Alfred A. Knopf.

Herskovits, Melville, J. ((1960), *Economic Anthropology*. New York: Alfred A.
Knopf.

Knight, Frank, H. (1960), Anthropology and Economics. In: Herkovits, M.J.,
Economic Anthropology. New York: Alfred A. Knopf.

Lewis, W.A. (1962), Foreword. In: Epstein, T.S., *Economic Development and
Social Change in South India*. Manchester: Manchester University Press.

Lipton, M. (1968), Interdisciplinary Studies in Less Developed Countries. In:
Journal of Development Studies.

McNamara, Robert, S. (1972), *Address to the Board of Governors.* Washington World Bank Group.

Marshall, A. (1936), *Principles of Economics.* 8th Ed. London.

Moore,M. (1974), 'The Logic of Interdisciplinary Studies', in: *Journal of Development Studies*, Vol.II, No. 4, April.

Sahlins, M.D. (1960), Political Power and the Economy in Primitive Society. In: Dole, J.E. & Carneiro, R.L. (eds.), *Essays in the Science of Culture in Honor of Leslie A. White.* New York: Crowell.

Salisbury, R.F. (1962), *From Stone to Steel.* London and New York: Cambridge University Press.

Seers, D. (1969), *The Meaning of Development.* IDS: Communication Series No. 44.

Spate, O.H.K. (1973), To Him that Hath Much. In: Epstein, T.S., *South India: Yesterday, Today and Tomorrow — Mysore Villages revisited.* London: MacMillan.

*Can an interdisciplinary approach make for better anthropology ? An inter-
disciplinary approach implies the acquisition by anthropologists of basic skills
in other fields. Geoffrey Masefield discusses relationships between anthropologists and agriculturalists. He shows why agricultural knowledge is important.
He sees fruitful areas for cooperation. Masefield suggests that anthropologists
should become technically literate in agriculture. To bear out his point of view
he shows how lack of knowledge about his field has weakened the work of
several anthropologists.*

ANTHROPOLOGY AND AGRICULTURAL EXTENSION WORK

G. B. Masefield

For almost fifty years now, lip-service has been paid to the idea that agricultural extension workers in developing countries should have some awareness of the anthropological circumstances surrounding them.. Form the nineteen-twenties onwards, probationers for the British colonial agricultural service doing a preliminary course at Cambridge University were compulsorily required to read only two books other than agricultural ones; one was Lord Lugard's 'Dual Mandate in British Tropical Africa' and the other was an anthropological work selected from a short list of approved titles according to the region the probationer was interested in.

But even without such official pressure, an interest in anthropology among tropical agriculturists would have naturally arisen. There was hardly an officer of the agricultural services of any of the colonial Powers who did not find himself inevitably becoming an amateur anthropologist or sociologist as his experience taught him that the obstacles to agricultural development were at least as often social as they were technical. Nearly all of them made an effort to read books by anthropologists about the peoples amongst whom they were working, where such books were available. They might even have been willing to read articles in journals, but to be aware of these and to obtain them in the remote places where they worked was usually beyond their capacity.

One might think that the situation had changed since colonies became independent, in that most agricultural officers are now natives of the countries in which they work and might be expected to have more knowledge of the local society.. This however is very often not true when an officer is posted outside his own tribal area. Such postings are inevitably common where tribes are small, and are sometimes a deliberate policy of governments, and one for which some valid reasons can be adduced. The need for agricultural extension workers to be supplied with anthropological information therefore often remains as acute as ever.

Some of the effects of the anthropological situation on extension work are so obvious as to be immediately apparent. In West Africa, for example, over large areas all farmers live in villages ('nucleated settlements') from which they travel on foot or by bicycle to work their farms, though by no means every day and often only for rather short hours. In East Africa by contrast there are large areas in which every farmer lives in an isolated house on his own holding and villages do not exist. The effects of these two systems on agricultural extension work are very different. In the West African case, it is rarely that an extension worker can find the occupier of a bad farm actually working on it when he happens to pass by and he is therefore denied the opportunity to discuss soils, crops and animals on the spot where they can be examined; but the village system makes it easy to gather together an audience of farmers for a talk or a demonstration by the extension worker. In East Africa, it is much easier to find the farmer on his farm because he is there even when in his house, but it is much more difficult to collect the scattered clients at a central point for a pep-talk. Some would go further and say that these two contrasting situations have deeper though more indirect effects on extension work, e.g. that isolated farmers tend to be more conservative and village dwellers more progressive.

A similarly obvious connection between social arrangements and extension work exists in the case of many grazing areas. Over most of Africa it is the custom that land which is not under crops or fenced is available for grazing to any local stockowners. It is impossible in these circumstances for the extension worker to advise any single individual to spend money or effort on the improvement of open pastures used by his stock by such measures as irrigation, drainage or fertilizer use. If the individual does so, his neighbours' animals will move in and take advantage of the improved growth of grass, and he will get little reward for his effort. The extension worker therefore knows he has to concentrate on getting pastures fenced before they will be improved.

These are fairly obvious physical examples; but sometimes there are more subtle aspects of local society which have psychological effects on extension work. It used to be a common accusation by the British that the Malays of Malaya were 'lazy' farmers uninterested in improvement, and they were contrasted unfavourably in this respect with immigrant Malay farmers from Indonesia. Only a knowledge of Malay history enables one to realise that the Malays of Malaya do not primarily regard themselves as farmers at all. By tradition and preference they are seafarers (often making their living by piracy in the past) and fishermen. Farming was a distasteful secondary occupation, left largely to women and occasional idle hours; and it is not surpising that so little pride is taken in doing it well.

Apart from these general considerations, there are many cases where an intelligent use of anthropological knowledge has been made by extension workers in promoting particular schemes of agricultural development (though even so it has not always ensured success!). At the best, this knowledge is brought into play at the planning stage and before actual operations begin. Such a case occurred in Kenya, where Hughes Rice (1947) planned a programme of soil conservation work based on the pre-existing 'ngwatio' system of communal labour among the local people. In a scheme to settle some of the Fula cattle-owners in Sierra Leone, careful note was taken of their previous practices, and each family was allotted a ranch of one square mile on which the transition could be made gradually from these to a more productive agriculture (Murray, 1958). When a scheme for increased milk production was being considered in Ethiopia, account was taken at the planning stage of the problem of what would be done with the milk during the 56-day fast before Easter when devout adults cannot consume milk (Batchelor, 1971). In such ways, increasing considera-tion has been given over the years to the social situation before undertaking agricultural developments, rather than running bald-headed into trouble after the scheme has begun, through sheer ignorance.

In slightly less favourable instances, mistakes have been recognised at a fairly early stage and rectified by suitable adjustments. Some years ago, short residential courses for practising farmers were started by the agricultural exten-sion service in Uganda. People to attend these courses were at first selected by extension officers on the basis of what appeared to be outstanding ability or interest. Such a process naturally threw up individuals from different areas, none of whom were usually near neighbours. Follow-up after the courses very soon revealed that most of these men soon gave up using any improved methods they had been taught and relapsed into the way of farming practised around them. It was diagnosed that three things were wrong:

a) isolated individuals soon forgot much of the detail learned on the course, whereas a group with the opportunity to discuss it together might have had a better collective memory.
b) isolated individuals attempting improvements which were not understood by those around them, and which often provoked scorn or hilarity, tended to lack the strength of mind to persist with them, whereas a neighbourhood group might have given each other moral support.
c) in some parts of the country, control of land use was in the hands of the extended family; a single, generally young, member of the family group could not alone make changes to suit the requirements for improved methods.

After this diagnosis was made, a different policy was adopted of selecting participants in courses by groups from close neighbourhoods, and in relevant cases as groups (usually of varied age and status) within extended families. It was found that, although this method resulted in fewer individuals of out-standing character being selected, the ultimate effects in farm improvement were greater than under the former policy.

Another instance of a problem arising, and being successfully dealt with, after an improvement scheme had already begun also comes from Uganda. In this case the agricultural extension service was urging farmers to give cropped land a periodic rest under planted grass to restore fertility. When a few farmers began to adopt this method, it was found that a problem arose with these grassed areas because other farmers claimed that, under customary law, land not actually planted with crops was available to the community either for free grazing (which in this case usually meant over-stocking and consequent erosion) or for re-allocation to other farmers who wished actually to plant crops. A solution was eventually found when the extension workers discussed the matter with the tribal chiefs, who decided that they could interpret the customary law so that planted grass was deemed to be a 'crop' and thereby given protection against encroachment.

Although there has thus been for a long time a general perception of the link between anthropology and agricultural extension work, the link came to be more publicly and formally recognised as time went on. This was particularly shown in some regional handbooks for extension workers produced in different parts of the tropics. Smith and Kruijer (1957) wrote a 'Sociological Manual for Extension Workers in the Caribbean'. 'A Handbook for Extension Workers' (Oloko *et al.*, 1961), prepared for use in Nigeria, opens with a long section described as 'Manual of Rural Sociology'. However, such publications have tended to confine themselves to trying to give extension workers an inkling of the content and importance of social anthropology without actually suggesting practical ways in which such knowledge can effect the success or failure of extension work. They have not, for example, stressed the importance of a concept put forward by some psychologists, which seems to me very basic to the success of extension work, that 'it is often easier to change the attitudes of small groups of people than those of a single individual' (Brown, 1963). It may be that to formulate such concepts is more the province of psychology than anthropology. But if the group approach is accepted as useful, the extension worker is surely entitled to ask the anthropologist for advise as to which groups (age groups, genetically related groups, neighbourhood groups, etc.) in a particular society would form the most appropriate channel for his message.

A particular angle which became recognised to have importance as extension methods grew more sophisticated was the conversational approach by the extension worker to the farmer. In many tropical societies there are set openings to conversations, rather as in a chess game, the observance of which is regarded as a part of normal good manners. There are conventional phrases of greeting, and conventional answers to them, sometimes to a depth of three or four remarks on either side. Next, it may be customary to ask whether rain has fallen locally, and whether peace prevails; one may go on to inquire about the health of the family and its relatives. Not until these preliminaries have been completed, and then often only slowly and obliquely, does one get around to disclosing the real purpose of why one is speaking to a person at all. All this has been put into words by a former Director of Agriculture of Tanganyika (Soper, 1959):

'The initial breaking of the ice is not an easy task. Patience is one of the first essentials: the main theme should seldom be introduced into conversation at an early stage — it may even have to be left until a second visit. Courteousness and a knowledge of local customs are also vital necessities in an extension officer'.

There is no doubt that in the past many Africans have been offended by what seems to them the brusque and ill-mannered form of speech of Europeans, including extension workers, who were unfamiliar with local codes. Frustrating as it may be to the extension worker to have to delay his message, we now understand that better results are often achieved by doing so.

In this as in other manifestations of the anthropology-extension link, it is important to recognise that the same considerations very often apply in advanced societies as in primitive ones. I once asked an experienced agricultural advisory officer in England to give me an outline of his day's procedure for a round of farm visits. He said that, before setting out at all, he always leafed through the latest issue of the local newspaper to cull news of recent social or sporting events in the parishes he was to visit. This gave him some starting-point for conversations with farmers which helped to integrate him into local society and put them at their ease before he began to discuss farming problems with them.

In all the instances given so far, the importance of a knowledge of 'local customs' was sooner or later realised and put to sensible use in furthering extension work. But there have also of course been many instances where an extension campaign has been completely stultified by the extension workers' ignorance of such customs. Two very typical instances come from Nigeria and both concern an important cash crop, the oil palm. Here the advice to plant oil palms of high-yielding varieties, instead of collecting fruit from low-yielding wild palms, was at first resisted by local chiefs on the ground that it would lead to claims of individual tenure of land and thus undermine tribal authority. A little later, the introduction of oil presses and of nut-cracking machnines to obviate the laborious manual methods of preparing oil and kernels was bitterly resisted by the women because it was they who had previously done the manual work and had earned by it useful cash which custom allowed them to keep for themselves.

Another example of frustration through ignorance was a personal disappointment to me when I was a young and inexperienced agricultural officer in Uganda, newly-posted to a remote district among an unfamiliar tribe. I was instructed by Government to open the first agricultural experiment station in the district, and was provided with money to purchase, amongst other things, the best local cattle I could find for a foundation herd with which to practise selective breeding. I bought some young bulls without difficulty, but then found that, such was the social prestige attached to owning numbers of cattle, no stockowne in the district would sell any female animals capable of producing offspring, still less the best ones. Eventually I acquired a herd in which half the female animals had had to be bought outside the district and were therefore unacclimatised, and the remainder were stunted, maimed or thought by their owners to be barren — hardly a good start for what was intended to be a model herd to be further improved by intelligent breeding.

I suppose that if I had been more experienced and realised the situation, I could have begun a lengthy campaign of persuading the chiefs of the value of an experimental herd in the hope that they would influence some owners to sell — but this in fact would have been impractical since the government allocation of funds expired at the end of the financial year, and would not have been likely to be renewed merely on a plea of anthropological necessity! No anthropologist had at that time published any work about the tribe concerned, so that this means of informing myself or Government was not open to me. It might again be thought that my own native staff ought to have advised me before I made a fool of myself by trying to buy cows; but, as any anthropologist will realise, their code of manners would never have allowed them to offer unsought advice to someone who was hierarchically their superior. All I can say is, that one does learn in time, and I should not have made the same mistake twenty years later. But there ought to be a method of re ducing this time-lag, and it is especially important that there should be in these days when so many agricultural 'experts' go to a tropical country for a year or two only, and have not time laboriously to acquire anthropological knowledge by personal experience.

Besides cases of this kind, where the failure of extension work is due to ignorance or mistake rather than intention, there are also of course instances of an anthropological kind where a deliberate influence is working against the success of extension work. A district agricultural officer in Tanganyika, whose report on the agriculture of the district in 1937 is probably still on the files of the district office, wrote in it that

'The chiefs and headmen are unprogressive and cannot be induced to give a lead
to their people. Their interests are largely in cattle and they take little interest in
the land . . . Much of the troubles of the district can be traced back to the poor
general diet . . . The witch doctors usually try to turn new developments to their
own advantage, but more serious is the mistrust of medical treatment which
they actively spread in order to safeguard their own interests'.

Another case in my own experience was in a district in Uganda where great influence was wielded by an 'oracle' whose sayings were circulated surreptitiously. These sayings purported to be spoken by the disembodied head of a long-dead chieftainess or goddess of the tribe. They covered many subjects but always had a strong anti-government flavour, and what she said should not be done the people would not do. In such circumstances, of course, there is little that an extension worker can do about it; but it is at least helpful if he is aware of what is going on and can channel the extension effort into other fields where it will not be so fruitless.

Since cases plainly do still arise where agricultural extension workers are not aware of anthropological information which would be helpful to them, what can be done to remedy this situation? There are probably failures of communication on both sides, and some of them are not really anybody's fault. There are, for instance, still vast areas in the tropics inhabited by peoples who have not been studied by any anthropologist. Or if they have been studied, the studies have not been published in book form and exist only in journals which are not available in the remote places which are usually concerned. In other cases, the only published anthropological descriptions may date from fifty or sixty years ago; they are often quite helpful, but from the point of view of an extension worker can sometimes be positively misleading because conditions or the outlook of the people have changed so much since then. These early books moreover were written at a time when anthropology was only an infant science. Many were written by missionaries or travellers with no professional training in anthropology at all. They often therefore suffer from defects or omissions which would not be found in the works of modern anthropologists, and are so much the less useful.

Another trouble is that, to agriculturalists, most books by anthropologists seem to describe societies as static, at a particular point in time, whereas one of the things the extension worker most wants to know is in what directions change is taking place, so that he can try to devise farming improvements which go along with these tendencies rather than swim against the tide. A typical example is the various forms of communal agricultural labour which used to be so common in Africa. Many extension workers have bethought themselves of trying to take advantage of this, and harnessing this apparently innate tendency of the African to enterprises such as 'group farming' and the co-operative movement. But experience with such schemes has in general been very disappointing, and many agriculturists have concluded that in Africa the tide is setting too strongly from communalism to individualism to attempt to stem it. There are many other experiences which have taught tropical agriculturists that 'putting the clock back' to a revival of older practices is one of the most difficult and frustrating of all extension operations. If older practices have real agricultural value and deserve to be followed, it is best for psychological reasons to dress them up as something new, which will appeal to people who like to think of themselves as progressive.

Another and rather closely related instance of change is the tendency, observable over so much of Africa, for communal land tenure slowly to give way to individual. This process has reached different points in different areas. A fascinating study of how this gradually happened in a district of Uganda and of how, at first furtively and then ever more openly, individual tenure came by an infinitesimal gradation of precedents to be accepted into the customary law, has been published by Fleming (1961). The author is a lawyer, and demonstrates incidentally how much in this case the trained legal outlook can enlighten the studies of both anthropologists and agriculturists.

If I venture to refer to another way in which agriculturists find much descriptive work by anthropologists to be wanting, I can only do it by being critically frank. I hope my anthropologist friends will forgive me; I can but plead that the forms of writing to which I refer do in sum amount to a considerable irritant between two disciplines which ought to be in the closest contact, and that I believe this can best be alleviated by open discussion.

Let us start with an irritant to agriculturists in anthropological works which is a minor though a continual one. This is the way in which anthropologists refer to plant and animal organisms. They seldom seem to succeed in arriving at a name which is acceptable to biologists of any category, and very often don't arrive at one which is recognisable at all. At the lower end of the scale we have the anthropologist who refers to a plant as 'a certain weed'. This to a biologist hardly seems to make it worth mentioning at all; but it is at least a frank admission of ignorance, though this could have been rectified by taking the plant to the nearest government agricultural office, such as existed in his time within a few miles of where he was working. It is worse, because positively misleading, when the same author describes another plant as 'a small green tomato called *njagi*'. 'Njagi' in the local language means a plant which is not a tomato at all; had it been a tomato, it would have raised very controversial questions about the distribution of the tomato at that time. Another anthropologist of very high repute mentions five insects on one page, all of which have some effect on the life of the people. The names of two are printed in italics and are presumably in the local language, though that is not stated; they are meaningless to any reader who does not know that rather obscure language (and subject always to doubt, because so many tropical peoples use the same word to describe several similar but different organisms). The third name is printed between inverted commas and appears to be in some other non-English language, though one cannot guess what. A fourth, in italics with a capital, is the correct Latin name of a genus of insects, but does not give the species. The fifth name is 'the common black fly', and one is left guessing as to which of many flies of black colour which are common on the world scale, on the African scale, or in that region of Africa, is meant. The works of the same author are (no doubt quite unintentionally) irritating to agricultural scientists because he uses spellings which are in their science old-fashioned and long superseded, such as 'oecology' for 'ecology' and 'savannah' for 'savanna', while he also uses technical terms which are strictly defined by them such as 'savanna' and 'horticulture' in senses which they would not accept.

A more serious irritant is what seems to agriculturists so often to be the unscientific way in which anthropologists write. There is only space here to give a couple of examples. One writer points out that the people observed work for longer hours on their farms during the rainy season because 'on cool cloudy days it is possible to work right up till noon'. The implication that it is not possible in the dry season is unscientific and misleading on a subject (working hours on tropical farms, and climatic stress) on which much exact information has been collected by agricultural and medical workers. Some individuals in this very tribe do sometimes work till noon in the dry season, and many farmers in other parts of the tropics do so in worse climatic conditions. What this author meant to say is that 'on cool cloudy days farmers are willing to work right up till noon'.

In my other instance, an anthropological writer seems needlessly to go out of his way to invite agricultural criticism. He writes of the people he is describing 'it may be doubted whether they could cultivate any crops other than those they now sow, without extensive irrigation in the dry season'. Since their staple crop was sorghum, than which many crops are more drought-resistant, five minutes' conversation with the local government agronomist would have showed him that there is no doubt at all that they could cultivate a dozen other crops, some of which are already grown not very far away. I am afraid that the reaction of agriculturally trained readers to this style of writing is that if anthropologists wish to be regarded as scientists (and agriculturists are not very sure whether they do — perhaps it would help to clarify this point too), then they must learn to write a bit more scientifically.

Another disappointment to agricultural readers is the apparent lack of general knowledge of tropical agriculture among so many anthropological writers. Many of them give long descriptions of the way in which a particular crop grows (one explains that a sweet potato 'is a tuberous crop') and how it is sown and harvested by the people whom they are observing, apparently blissfully unaware that these are general tropical practices, in no way particular to that people, and usually much more fully and accurately described already in agricultural textbooks on the cultivation of that crop. Conversely they often fail to provide just the information which agriculturists would like to have from them, of unusual practices in cultivating a crop which really are unique to that people. They also frequently fail to point out, perhaps because they so often work in small areas, interesting differences in agricultural methods which occur within the area inhabited by the same tribe. Thus the two chief anthropological accounts of the Baganda tribe, both of which purport to cover its whole territory, devote in both cases much space to the cultivation of their staple food crop, the plantain, but neither observes the many and interesting differences in its treatment in diferent areas.

This however, is not so surprising to agriculturists as the apparent ignorance of so many anthropologists about the general historical background of tropical agriculture. This applies particularly to knowledge of the history of crop dispersal around the world. Several anthropologists who have described crop production by peoples in eastern Africa seem to have been unaware that some of the crops they were dealing with had been cultivated there for 1,000 years and others (originally of American origin) for only about 200. Thus they missed the point that many ancient customs and ceremonies are attached to the growing of the former group, and hardly any to the latter. Again, an anthropological writer who makes many references to the great outbreak of rinderpest in tropical Africa in the eighteen-nineties writes as if he did not know that it was so destructive because it was the first of its kind, and was started by a movement of herds following the Italian invasion of Ethiopia in 1890. Such apparent ignorance is a disappointment to agriculturists, who in general expect anthropologists to have a better knowledge of history than they have themselves.

What then do agriculturists ask of anthropologists? I don't know that they can define all their wants, but some at least are clear even if it is not certain that anthropologists can satisfy them. One phenomenon, puzzling to agriculturists and a problem in extension work with which anthropologists might be able to help, has arisen in the following manner. In the early days of agricultural science in the tropics, European scientists tended to draw on their experience in temperate lands to dictate to tropical farmers how they should grow their crops. It was in time realised that this procedure often made nonsense in the tropical environment, and that in fact the farmers had much to teach the scientists as well as *vice versa*. A practice therefore arose of extension workers questioning tropical farmers in great detail as to how they grew their crops. These questions were usually addressed to elderly farmers, who were presumed to be the chief repositories of knowledge and experience. Since the elderly are usually the most garrulous of the human race (a fact not sufficiently stressed by anthropologists), the questions elicited a flood of replies. It became evident that these replies fell into two classes, a) those which seemed to show sufficient chance of enshrining a grain of scientific truth to be worth testing by experiment, b) those which appeared to be based on arrant nonsense.

The differance can perhaps best be explained by concrete examples. I was once asking a farmer in Uganda about his choice of banana varieties for planting, and was told two things. One was that certain varieties were more liable to be blown over by wind than others and therefore he never planted them in exposed situations; the other was that certain varieties were more likely to be struck by lightning than others, and therefore he never planted them near his house. Of these two statements, the first seems well worth testing by experiment, and the second extremely unlikely to be true. But such beliefs and statements are not limited to tropical peoples. I remember two things which I was told by an old and uneducated English gardener. The first was that in digging holes in grassland for planting fruit trees, I should turn the top sod upside down and place it in the bottom of the hole; this seemed to make sense, because it would improve drainage and supply organic nutrients to the roots of the tree. The second was that 'peas don't like old pea-sticks', and I should use new pea-sticks each year. This I guessed to be nonsense, and my guess was later confirmed by my perfectly satisfactory experience of using old pea-sticks.

Discrimination between the two classes of reply is very important, because of the time and expense involved in testing such statements by experiment. In Trinidad, two scientists spent considerable time and published a research paper on their experiments to test a belief held by local farmers that bamboo poles should not be cut while the moon is waxing because they will then be more subject to insect attack; their tests showed this belief to be unfounded (Kirkpatrick and Simmonds, 1958). I myself once spent part of a year testing a belief of some farmers in eastern England that two-year old bean seed is better than 'new' seed; this also turned out to be erroneous. Any help that anthropologists could offer in trying to sort out statements derived from real experience from those based on myth would be extremely welcome to agriculturists.

A rather similar problem in agricultural extension work is that of apparently unfounded rumours about farming phenomena which seem to have no basis in fact. During the nineteen-forties a great deal of extension work in Africa was concerned with soil conservation. A measure, new to the people, which was urged on them by extension officers in several countries was that root crops such as sweet potatoes and cassava (manioc) should be planted in continuous ridges laid out along the contour to prevent erosion. In Uganda, many farmers refused to do this because they alleged that if it were done, rats would burrow continuously along the ridge and eat the whole crop of roots. In Nyasaland people also refused to adopt this practice because they said that the ridges would become water-logged and the tubers would rot. A feature common to both cases was that, although the rumours were widely believed and used as a reason for non-compliance with extension advice, no one could be found who had actually observed the alleged phenomena; all had 'heard of it from friends'. If any anthropologist can suggest where and how such rumours start, it would help extension workers who would like to predict and prevent them.

Many special problems, on which the advice of anthropologists would be welcome, arise in the sphere of famine relief with which government agricultural staff are often concerned. One is the breakdown of morality, a well-known result of starvation, which so often leads to the theft of produce and of standing crops or animals on pastures. Firth (1959), one of the few anthropologists who have recorded observations on a famine situation, writes of a famine in a Pacific island that 'Almost the only people who did not steal at the height of the famine were the chiefs and members of their families'. For those who have to arrange precautions such as the guarding of crops and livestock, it would be helpful to have more information about the stage at which stealing is begun and by what elements in society. In a drought in Zululand which had killed off the local cattle, supplies of liquid milk sent into the area were rejected because of the custom that a Zulu may only drink milk from cows that belong to a kinsman. Dried milk powder ultimately proved acceptable; but time and health might have been saved if anthropological advice on this aspect had been available earlier.

Another very intractable problem in famine relief is the maldistribution of relief foods within families. It is of little use relief organisations straining themselves to provide specially nutritious food for infants or expectant and nursing mothers, if when distributed to households these merely find their way, as so often happens in tropical societies, into the mouth of the male head of the family. The opposite happened in some occupied European countries which were very short of food in the second world war; parents denied themselves even the minimum amount of food necessary for them to do a productive day's work, in order to give their children the best diet available. Not everybody can be fed at communal centres; expert social knowledge is needed to predict and amend family eating behaviour. A start could be made towards recognising and solving such problems if governments would commission anthropologists to study social behaviour during famines and would include their reports as part of the official report on the famine which is generally produced afterwards.

In these remarks I have perhaps concentrated, but if so not without purpose, on what may seem to be rather minor matters. This is because I believe it is the sum total of a large number of minor matters which most impedes fruitful collaboration between anthropologists and agriculturists. The big problems obtrude themselves, and nobody of any experience can be unaware of them. Everybody has realised, for instance, for many years that farmers who have had previous experience of irrigation will derive much more benefit from an expensive government irrigation scheme than those who have not, and that this is a major reason for the relative success of the Gezira scheme in the Sudan and the relative failure of the Middle Niger scheme in West Africa. What is needed is to determine the social reasons why farmers not previously versed in irrigation find such difficulty in taking advantage of it. If anthropologists could analyse such problems, then it would be the duty of agriculturists to try to find solutions for them which they would again check with the anthropologists as being acceptable. That would be co-operation indeed.

References

Batchelor, P.G. (1971), Menz Team, Ethiopia. Rural Life *16*, No. 3, p. 17.

Brown, J.A.C. (1963), Techniques of Persuasion. London.

Firth, R. (1959), Social Change in Tikopia. London.

Fleming, J.T. (1961), Recent Developments in Customary Kisoga Land Tenure. Entebbe, Uganda.

Kirkpatrick, T.W. and N.W. Simmonds (1958), Bamboo Borers and the Moon. Trop. Agriculture, Trin. *35*, 299.

Murray, A.K. (1958), The Fula Cattle Owners of Northern Sierra Leone, their Cattle and Methods of Management. Trop. Agriculture, Trin. *35*, 102.

Oloko, T., H.L. Dusenberry and D.W. Pett (1961), A Hand-Book for Extension Workers. University College, Ibadan, Nigeria.

Rice, J.Hughes (1947), Soil Conservation Organisation in Fort Hall District as Adapted from the Indigenous 'Ngwatio' System. E. Afr. Agric. Journal *12*, 200.

Smith, M.G. and G.J. Kruijer (1957), Sociological Manual for Extension Workers in the Caribbean. University College of the West Indies.

Soper, J. (1959), Extension Work in Agriculture. Corona *11*, 214.

What is the value of legal anthropology undertaken by anthropologists who have not acquainted themselves with the elements of legal training? Duncan Derrett has worked closely with anthropologists. He feels very strongly that they should have legal training. Derrett gives examples of important legal matters where the special skills of legal anthropologists might help people who need assistance. The paper is important in that it identifies intellectual and human constraints on the growth of interdisciplinary anthropology. Derrett emphasizes that lawyers need anthropology just as anthropology needs lawyers.

THE ROLES OF LAW AND ANTHROPOLOGY IN DEVELOPMENT

J. Duncan M. Derrett

It may seem odd to a student of any third discipline that there should not have been researchers trained in *both* anthropology and law. I know of only one (double) graduate in laws who has gone over to anthropology, and his results await publication. The leading journal for juridical ethnology is the *Zeitschrift für vergleichende Rechtswissenschaft*. Among its very numerous studies of law in or the laws of, underdeveloped peoples, I have not detected one written by a trained lawyer who has qualified himself in anthropology. There are typical legal minds, and typical anthropological minds, and there seem to be no cases of more than mediocre examples of the one submitting himself for actual retraining at the hands of professed paragons of the other.[1] Lawyers who turn over to political science are not rare, and as political scientists they have to handle material suitable for the anthropologogist: but field work done in an anthropological manner would be beyond their inclinations and their timetable.

Lawyers are typically men with little *abstract* quality: they are not detected, when at school, as likely to make any particular contribution to music, literature, history, mathematics, etc. They are practical people, keen to be helpful citizens, to figure (perhaps) on the public stage as advocates, keen to display their gift of 'common sense' before admiring audiences, but impatient of serious enquiries why their craft should exist, why they are necessary. The facts that they do exist, that clients need to be advised and defended, and that practitioners need to learn, to be taught, and to be constantly retaught in the craft, suffices to explain them. The unedifying relationship between legislature, judiciary, practitioners, and the client-public is never exposed for the haphazard, unscientific, empirical thing that it is — it would be bad taste.

Lawyers are often pompous, self-important, empirical, pragmatic, and little-cultured people: and their occasional affectations of cultured hobbies, and

---

1) An example, Derrett, ed., *Studies in the Laws of Succession in Nigeria*, (Oxford University Press 1965). The distance between anthropological interest and legal language is emphasized tartly in reviews by Edwin Ardener in *African Affairs*, April 1967, p. 166, and Brian Harvey at *Modern Law Review* 30 (1966), 237-8.

their development of the art of self-expression (in their clients' interests) which sometimes brings them renown, serve only to emphasize the point. Sensitiveness to actual movements in the human spirit, as constrasted with ephemeral reactions to political or economic changes, would not be expected of them, nor would they be sufficiently patient to inquire into them. Their occasional bursts into song about 'Law' only serve to reveal the loquacious lawyer's lack of self-awareness and his pragmatism. They are more at home describing 'famous cases' for the public's amusement. What the public actually *do* interests them only in so far as it brings them business, e.g., if it can come within the definition of a crime; or it affords material for entertainment.

One would go to a lawyer to learn what the law actually is on any matter, and what is likely to be handed down by a final court of appeal. Prognosticators of the practical, lawyers are also curiously irresponsible: no one of them accepts responsibility for the law as it is, though law reform agencies (made up primarily of academics) do make suggestions on the basis of research when formally commissioned to do so; but statistics of what actually happens (e.g. the murder rate, abortion rate) typically interest them much less than what are the corresponding laws in other jurisdictions. The fact that they are known (at least in England) to consult 'social scientists' (they do not employ them permanently) in such contacts confirms their own refusal to be educated in such techniques. I am reminded of two incidents. I once spoke of a forthcoming judgement to a barrister whose junior I was in the case. He replied: 'I do not care if the judgement is right provided we win!' And I once asked if I could consult a Supreme Court judge about an important piece of social legislation then grossly agitating the public. He said: 'I do not want to be bothered with questions of pending legislation. I have quite enough trouble with statutes when they are actually passed.' That sufficiently shows the mentality. Lawyers remind me (in short) of fashion-servers such as shoemakers, who must ply a craft without a direct influence on the movement of fashion or its content.

Anthropologists seem to have their own shortcomings. All of them seem to be educated in big ideas. They like 'bold conceptualizations'. They will see the habits of the Mbongo-Mbongo as throwing indispensable light on Life, Death, and Eternity. It is not an accident that their 'interference' in the realm of jurisprudence is confined to very broad propositions, in which they are not notably succesful. They make more or less hasty identifications of an institution or rule which they find in the field with a more or less comparable rule discovered from some legal textbook. Their work may be typified by a contrast published by A. N. Allott, himself a (double) graduate in laws influenced by anthropological thinking because of its appropriateness and (if I may say so) its sheer inevitability until quite recently in any context of African law. Allott quotes[2] Robert F. Gray[3] in an unnecessary attempt to make a definition of the word 'family':

> '. . . the composite picture of the family that we come out with is something like this: an ephemeral, non-structural group; located in the domestic domain of society, which comprises a system of integrating relations; almost universal by virtue of the utility of its constituent relationships; variable in composition and devined by aspects of certain functions which it serves. As a working definition, this is a rather unwieldly formulation upon which to base systematic analysis. It does reflect a general dissatisfaction with older conceptions and a veering away from the idea of a single institution or a static structure. Evidently the concept of 'family', as now employed in social anthropology, cannot be encompassed in a simple definition. In that case it might be approached in some other way, perhaps as a nexus of certain processes.'

The lawyers who might read this discussion would immediately ask for what purpose such a definition is required — since in their own craft all definitions are *ad hoc* and at every step care is taken to see that definitions do not impose rigidity upon a emerging rule which the public interests requires. Allott, however, offers a definition of his own which is perhaps not intended to be of value to lawyers, since it contains undefined terms, and has vague expressions which would create more practical difficulties than they could ever solve:

> 'A family group is a relatively stable, structured association of individuals, linked principally by blood relationships but also in part by affinal and residential ties, and having a range of shared economic and social functions.'

Lawyers find anthropological works unreadable unless they are anecdotal, for even when they are about law they do not deal with ascertained rules enforced by recognizable tribunals. Anthropologists evidently find legal works (unless airily jurisprudential) unreadable because they have too many detailed rules in them, interconnected in terms of a system of thought which is obviously fictional. Anthropologists who have tackled legal topics have generally done so *historically*, so as to keep well clear of any actual problem and its solution.[4]

I have worked alongside anthropologists for a quarter of a century and no one ever wanted to learn from me, for more than five minutes, anything I could teach in the field of Sanskrit Law, or modern Hindu law, though I was far from being a typical law teacher[5], and no human alternative has

2) At *Zeitschrift für vergleichende Rechtswissenschaft* 71/2 (1970), p. 107.
3) In R. F. Gray and P. H. Gulliver, ed. *The Family Estate in Africa* London 1964).
4) E.g. B. Cohn 'Some notes on law and change in N. India', in: P. Bohannan, ed., *Law and Warfare* (Garden City, N.Y., Natural History Press, 1967), pp. 139-59.
5) Invitations to speak at home and abroad on my subject always led to hostile comment

offered himself. When challenged to explain why this was so, delinquents always offered the same excuse, viz. that the anthropologist is not concerned with what *was* the law, nor with lawyers' versions of what the law is ideally (as the courts see it), but with what actually goes on in people's minds. The real reason might be that the expert, who will acquire a smattering of his society's language in order to control his interpreter's functions for the short time he is in the 'field', has not the apparatus or the training to engage in systematic study of an ancient language, or to master intricate and voluminous legal materials which normally make sense only to a person operating on a different intellectual wavelength. One cannot, of course, complain if a 'literature' man does not want to learn law, nor a musician, nor a logician; but one can complain if the great exponents of cultural flexibility and intellectual adjustment are unable to demonstrate that very quality in a field where the two disciplines, law and anthropology, overlap. Perhaps this failure can be diminished if the two parties come to understand each other better.

As I understand the position, the anthropologist who is involved in development seeks to understand the current climate, culture, and social organization of the people whom he is studying. In so doing he is called upon the study questions like kinship, property, religion, and e.g. caste, not to speak of racial and inter-tribal relationships, which would lead the untrained mind so far from the central matters of investigation as to make the search unmanageable and unprofitable. He hopes to describe what he finds, to analyse (and even predict), and it is up to others what use (if any) they make of his discoveries. He has to be objective in his report, whilst sympathetic in his dealings with the objects of his investigation. He does not aim to *change* them, and occasionally feels compelled to 'protect' them from change. Political motives, to which the lawyer seems entirely subservient, threaten primitive peoples at every turn, and the anthropologist quite naturally finds himself opposed to them. After all, he does not attempt identification with the ruling elites from whom these political pressures stem. This is a tightrope stance, and only a highly trained anthropologist can achieve anything within this wide scope of reference. The evaluation and appreciation made by a man who has no fear or favour, who speaks without praise or blame, is a miracle in its own right. But if anthropologists have not learnt to empty themselves of subjective prejudice before they begin their work, who can be expected to achieve this?

from anthropologists; not that they objected to my matter, but always to my 'methodology'. The attitude of political scientists and historians to the identical presentation was markedly more receptive.

48

When we come to the task of discovering, exploring, mapping, and describing *custom*, no one is better equipped than the anthropologist, and it is to him that we look when a careful and well rounded report is required. We have already seen how one struggles to free himself from legal and 'legislative' chains to describe something which, in his own language, has no name. He is the man who ought to be employed to discover what custom obtains amongst a tribe or people. The pathetic desiccated questionnaires that are often circulated to obtain a mini-presentation of customary laws in a given territory (having hundreds of peoples) are more likely to elicit something approaching relevant and reliable information if they are drafted by anthropologists in liaison with lawyers.

Unfortunately the aims of anthropologists in the field are less often to help or benefit their informants than to build their own careers. Their reports are written up, not so much as independent contributions to knowledge on the people as they were found to be, but rather as demonstrations of the author's capacity to contribute to overarching theories of anthropology or methodology. This produces a subjectivity of its own. The anthropologist may despise the lawyer who hesitates to define even 'property', and who suspects all definitions outside the scope of the fictionally normative, which is *his* medium of communication. But what is the lawyer to make of the anthropologist to whom his 'subjects' are meaningful only so far as they subserve his own theoretical development? The lawyer watches an anthropologist describing toenail-biting amongst the Mbongo in the exclusive framework of Feet in Human Culture, and sees in this exercise at once the pretentious and the fraudulent.

Momentarily we might consider the situation of the missionary. The mission field is a place where principles of theology are applied. Missionaries are often involved in places and in tasks meaningful to the anthropologist. The latter seldom knows which to abhor more, the missionary or the lawyer. Overarching systematic considerations influence not only the theologians' description of what he sees in his raw material, but also his method of enquiring into his material. Missionaries have an intense personal interest in those amongst whom they work, imputing to the latter the benefit of an excercise which is, in psychological terms, functional chiefly for the missionary himself. In this he is similarly placed with the anthropologist, his rival in methodology and in goals. It is significant that as the drive to obtain converts diminishes, intellectual sympathy with the cultures of the 'heathen' has increased. The missionary struggles to understand his prospective flock, and their existing religions, under the handicap that the more sympathetically he studies them (e.g. Verrier Elwin's career) the further he moves from chances of converting them: he may be converted himself.[6] He tries to *induce in* them (whereas the lawyer

6) The classic example of commitment to India in order to propagate the gospel is

more often *imposes upon* them) normative schemes foreign to them at the moment of first contact. And, in this attempt, he brings them and their current condition into confrontation with his own intellectual formation. Poles apart in their aims, the anthropologist and the missionary are alike in exploiting a people susceptible to their investigations for the development of their personal concepts and the effecting of their own schemes. Whatever can be said against what the lawyer does it is hardly this. Unconscious bias is not less insidious than conscious bias, and missionaries and anthropologists can be accused of both; however they readily detect each others'. The former has the advantage at least in this, that he does not chose his field, and his theme, to suit fashion and the flow of academic publishers' requirements.[7]

The aim of the practising lawyer, on the other hand, is to make money and to be an influential (responsible) man. The lawyer is South Asia is very much a businessman and lives by advertisement and touting.[8] The stated aims, to right wrongs and protect the weak, are convenient 'front' propositions intended to reconcile the community to the price they pay for his services. The aim of most academic lawyers, besides earning their living (like anyone else) is to train future practitioners and thus to pass on a useful craft, and not unoften to do so in an atmosphere and with techniques which will be educationally respectable (i.e. with a high dgree of abstraction) and will convey a veneer of culture without demanding that the pupils show evidence of being cultured. The academic is forced to generalise and to speculate beyond his material, which he does not control, and which comes to him (in the forms of statutes and case-law) as heaps of rough, unpolished stones, which he attempts (with the aid of his colleagues) to reduce to a more congruous mass than a heap of polished pebbles. And before he has done this, some have exploded, some disintegrated, and others, as unmanageable, have taken their places.

The academic becomes impatient of the practitioner, who is tied, at the drop of a hat, to any practical problem which may chance to emerge, ready to argue equally effectively, on successive days, opposite cases even before the same judge: the practitioner is impatient with the academic (except,

that of R. De Nobili: V. Cronin, *A Pearl to India* (London, Hart-Davis, 1959). The ethos and ways of the missionary during the imperial period are exemplified in N. C. Sargant and A. M. Ward, *W. E. Tomlinson* (Madras, etc., U.S.C.L., 1952). The wheel is coming full circle, as we see from the splendid Klaus Klostermaier, *Hindu and Christian in Vrindaban* (London, S.C.M. Press, 1969).
7) Until recently few books in the field of anthropology failed to have the words 'social change' in their titles.
8) The competitive and parasitic atmosphere of law practice is well brought out by C. Morrison, 'Munshis and their Masters . . .', *J. Asian St.* 31/2 (1972), 309-28.

perhaps, the man who drilled him in particular rules which he still requires in his practice) for his concern with abstract reconciliations of divergent matter which cannot always be of direct use in preparing a brief or addressing a judge or a jury. Neither is, in his function, concerned for the people whose law is being considered, and what the law ought to be (apart from the occasional sarcasm, in the nature of light relief) is solemnly banished from lecture-room and court-room alike. A written critique of chapters of law is of no interest to practitioners and most of their teachers, especially in India and Pakistan. It is not the *professional* aim of an anthropologist to prevent change in his 'society', nor to protect his 'friends' from the ravages of 'development'. If he speaks as if it were it is the man speaking not the anthropologist. Similarly it is the lawyer's aim to know the law and plot its course, to help it to work in resolving disputes and anticipating them, and to work in, with, and through it. It is not his task to change it, nor to protect it from change. The typical 'conservatism' of the lawyer is not a matter of his resisting change, so much as his insistence, before students (if he is a teacher) and judges, that this is the law (as he would say 'this is my life'). If the law is changed by the Supreme Court, or the House of Lords, he at once, without shame, hesitation, or consciousness of any anomaly, tells the very same students, and the very same judge, that the law has changed; and he is as strongly 'for' it as he was for yesterday's law which was wrong: he has no personal attachment to any rule, only to his function. This is not intellectual flexibility, as men versed in literature, divinity, or even history might suppose. It is the natural reaction of the practical man to new discoveries which work experimentally. The courts are the laboratory, and he no more works in yesterday's law than a chemist uses outdated formulas or a physician prescribes outmoded remedies.

The craft of the law includes *imposing* and *imputing*. Both must be understood, and both are deplored by the anthropologist. Since the legal system operates to facilitate law, order, and peace and prosperity amongst the inhabitants it must subserve the needs of the generality of people, and the rules which are inherited or enacted or developed by the judiciary are intended to produce direct and indirect effects suitable to the general good. Even the anthropologist, if struck on a vital part by an assailant who pleads that he is not to be accountable for the effects of his act, will understand the law's entirely fictional imputation to the assailant of an intention to maim or kill, without strict proof of what his intention was. Even an anthropologist will find the validity of favourable laws (e.g. fiscal laws raising taxes from which he himself is supported) healthfully upheld by the fiction that the legislature meant what it is reported as saying, even though each and every legislator present when the bill was passed could be brought to testify on oath that his intention at the time was otherwise. The construction (as it is called) of deeds, wills, and statutes proceeds upon lines of convention paying little or no attention, or (if at all) only subject to very strict rules, to the actual and provable intentions of the parties apart from the works actually used. The law thus imputes to people intentions which they cannot be proved to have had, as well as intentions they are not allowed to prove that they *did not* have. And simple peoples with few or no rules can find themselves subject to statute and case-law with all the complexities of a highly developed society, because it is conclusively presumed that once they are subject to a law, its validity will not be affected by their ignorance of it or lack of use for it (for the time being). Thus, old, and sometimes even imported, doctrines of partnership law will be imposed upon people cooperating within a loose framework which they themselves have never identified, let alone named. And all this in the name of regularity, impartiality, and certainty. The legal fiction is the best known type of fiction: it is found to work and that is its justification. Naturally, except for the anthropological student of fictions, this thought-world is abhorrent to non-lawyers.

The anthropologist, on the other hand, when he comes to the Law, comes to find out what it is on the ground. He is not surveying lawyers. He identifies, rather, and describes a local *custom*. Law is served by lawyers; custom may, and may not, be served by elders or other recognised repositories of customary law and lore. It is not surprising that wherever the political authority is persuaded that custom must rule uninterrupted lawyers are excluded from the elders' deliberations. Vain hope! The elders are all too curious about what is decided relevant to their customs by some official body. The elders become, after a fashion, lawyers in their turn. For the anthropologist the decrees of courts are of interest as specimens of court-activity. But anthropologists never research into the anthropology of courts! A mass of detail exists on lawyers, judges, their ways of life, especially in the developing countries where the drama is constant — but it is of interest (so far) only to social historians.[9]

For state courts belong to the imposed structure of the developed society, and have not yet been chosen as fields for anthropological enquiry. The

---

9) M. Galanter, 'An incomplete bibliography of the Indian legal profession', *Law & Society Review* 3/2-3 (1968-9), 445-62. A revealing biography of a cosmopolitan lawyer, not least Asian when he reminds us of the fact, is M. C. Setalvad, *My Life, Law and Other Things* (Bombay, Tripathi, 1970). The author was one of the most influential lawyers of his day (India's Attorney-General during the whole of the formative period of constitution building after Independence); development is a theme that never arises in his life or thought, except in the framework of the disputed constitutionality of expropriatory legislation, approached always from a technical angle.

anthropologist's law is therefore law-in-action and law-in-fact, the real existence
of obligations recognised and practised by his society, whether or not they
would be recognised and applied by courts in the sense demanded by that society. The findings of the anthropologist are not law in the lawyer's sense,
and the lawyer's law is not Law in the anthropologist's sense, or senses.

There are, however, numerous topics where anthropological investigation
is directly relevant, and should be carried out, not as scholar's exercises but
as a public service. These include family customs (with implications in the
realm of fiscal law, which imposes taxes upon families and individuals), customs of social cooperation (including election procedure), customs relating
to economic cooperation (including the topics beloved of political scientists
untouchability and protective discrimination)[10] and practices and thought-
patterns involved in religious institutions, particularly those which (because
of financial implications) have attracted the hostile attention of politicians
and absorbed the energies of lawyers.[11] Since law's chief weakness lies in
its progressive inefficiency and obsolescence, all programmes of law reform
relate directly to *change* at some level. And it is in marking, explaining, and
delimiting social change that the anthropologist can use his skills effectively,
while the lawyer has neither the time, the patience, nor the skill to make objective surveys (unless as a member of a commission this is allotted to him
as his task), or utilise their results. Yet his skill in sharpening and completing
a draft schedule of questions should always be of value to the one who actually makes the survey.

I therefore detect a hidden common aim. Lawyers need to amend the law
to achieve a determined political end, visualised against the background of
society's present condition and possible future movement. Their subservience
to political chiefs need not be assumed without qualification. The Whither
is often in practice qualified by the How, as we saw in the case where taxation
was eventually imposed on corporations operating outside territorial waters;
but that was an instance where (as often) politicians induced lawyers to think
again: it could be a two-way influence. Anthropologists, especially if they

10) M. Galanter, 'Group preferences and group membership in India', *J. As. Afr. St.*
2 (1967); the same, 'The abolition of disabilities – untouchability and the law', in
J. Michael Mahar, ed., *The Untouchables in Contemporary India* (Tucson, University
of Arizona Press, 1972), 228-314.
11) Derrett, 'The reform of Hindu religious endowments', in D.E.Smith, ed., *South
Asian Politics and Religion* Princeton University Press, 1966), ch. 14. The story of
a marvelous case of a fraudulent *mahant* (Amalendu Sen, 'The Tarakeswar Case . . .',
Law Quarterly (Calcutta), 9/2, 1972, 137-48) is instructive. The behavior of trustees
of endowments is well illustrated by *State of Gujarat v. Acharya* (1970) 74 Bombay
L.R. 155 (S.C.).

work in a field observed before, can see the effect of a law imposed from afar off, and can indicate what are the needs of the moment and the dangers of ill-informed legislation. They can warn as well as inform. For the remoter society's interests are never put to the judge who decides cases which are bound to affect them, except through coinsel who, like all lwayers, think in imposed or imputed categories, and are by defintion, biased and limited to their client's narrow, ephemeral interests. This is where the objective and continuing interest of the anthropologist can do good.

It goes almost without saying that no anthropologist will adopt the position that some part of the population is more 'enlightened' than another; the anthropological position, as I understand it, is that no customs are open to value judgements. However, drift, and the effect of imitation and emulation are certainly within the anthropologist's scope of vision, and he can report what percentage of instances now follow a pattern emerging elsewhere (as in the case of the constantly alleged 'break-up'! of the joint Hindu family), and this at once evades the dangers of 'codification' of custom and constitutes essential information for the would-be social and political planner.

One might therefore enquire what anthropological work has been done in India (and pre-1947 Pakistan), and what prevents more from being done. District gazetteers and censuses have gained much from work by professional and amateur anthropologists. Books entitled 'Castes and Tribes . . .' are available. Few of them were written by men whose qualifications would be recognised by anthropologists today. In Kerala and Madras the reports of anthropologists are sometimes used as expert testimony on law, of which the judges may take judicial notice: but there are those judges who claim that this is not admissible, since the qualifications of the anthropologists are doubtful and the objectivity and completeness of their reports is impugned.[12] Moreover the courts turn to anthropologists' reports only where *custom* is recognised by the law itself as a source of law, and where those that plead and rely on a custom are unable to prove it conclusively by living testimony from the people said to be governed by it, or by pointing to a conclusive[13] judgement of a law court holding that such a custom has been effectively proved.[14] Further, anthropologists alone can help when, as amazingly often,

12) Cf. *N. Kuttan* v. *N. Neelakandan* 1966 Kerala L.T. 790 with *Sheikriyammada N. Koya* v. *Administrator* 1967 K.L.T. 395 as discussed between P. Govindan Nair, J., and Isaac, J., in *Kali Pennamma* v. *St. Paul's Convent* 1972 K.L.T. 12. Anthropologists' reports were consulted in *Janardhanan* v. *Kaliamma* A.I.R. 1968 Mad. 105 and *Prabhu Sahay* v. *Junas* A.I.R. 1966 Pat. 430.
13) *Janardhanan* (see last note).
14) *Mat. Subhasi* v. *Nawab* (1940) 68 Ind. App. 1; *Suganchand* v. *Mangibai* I.L.R. 1942 Bom. 467; *Mst. Maro* v. *Paras Ram* A.I.R. 1966 H.P.22.

the peoples do not know what their customs are (but individuals will testify to any custom which their litigating comrade wants to be proved); and where the anthropologist's statement is supported by conflicting or inadequate evidence the court may give it up as hopeless, and indeed hold that there is no custom (so that the party relying on it loses his case).[15]

Continuing anthropological work is sporadic, private, and subject to all the accidents of particular studies. The government employs anthropologists in connection with the Scheduled Tribes and the Scheduled Castes (formerly Criminal Tribes, Untouchables, etc.).[16] But the work has little or no bearing on law, since these workers' reports do not look towards, nor have any relevance for. legal administration. The concern of the Government of India for tribal peoples cannot be denied (and the same may be said of Sri Lanka) and they are protected by special laws against exploitation, and much general law is not applied to them: but a detailed survey made of Santal law and custom by Mr. W. G. Archer, I.C.S., remains unpublished to this day. The general impression is that such tribal peoples must continue to apply their own customs to themselves in their haphazard way, as far as possible uninterfered with by the official courts. This diarchy may be satisfactory so far it goes, but can hardly last for ever. Meanwhile, the mass of the non-tribal public are subjected to the general law, in which they take an interest much as other peoples interest themselves in various forms of gambling, and without any careful enquiry at the neighbourhood level whether it is suitable for them. A digest of the customary laws of Kutch cannot be traced in any library know to me.[17]

The reform of Islamic law has been demanded for half a century at least. Amongst many anomalies and archaic features unfavourable attention has been drawn by the husband's power of divorcing his wife unilaterally, and of marrying up to four wives without committing the crime of bigamy. There are

15) *Kochan Kani* v. *Mathevan* A.I.R. 1971 S.C. 1398, or 1971 K.L.T. 458 (S.C.).
16) B. S. Bhargava, *The Criminal Tribes. A Socio-Economic Study of the Principal Criminal Tribes and Castes in Northern India* Lucknow, Universal Publishers, 1949). An unorthodox view of these people and their status appears in S. Venugopal Rao, *Facets of Crime in India* (Bombay, Allied Publishers, 1967). For the character of litigation in India see citations in Derrett, *History of Indian Law (Dharmasastra)* (Leiden, Brill, 1973), 14 n.l; also a revealing article at *Kerala Law Times*, 1973, Journal Section, 24-5.
17) This proves the total want of interest in this subject outside the immediate region: the book (*Digest of Local Customs in the Province of Kutch* published under the authority of H.H.The Maharao of Kutch) came to light for the first time in *Nandvana v. Sorathia* A.I.R. 1953 Kutch 4. The *Digest* has more than 645 sections! By contrast, intricate rules of equity law, unknown to any non-lawyer inhabitant, can be located instantly in any law library in South Asia, Britain, or America. I have never seen the *Hnam Dan* or *Mizo Customary Laws* compiled by government order by experts. It surfaced as a legal authority in *L. Rinkini* v. *Liansawna* A.I.R. 1973 Gau 116.

also curious features in the law of intestate succession which make it impossible to regard Islamic law as fit for the modern world. The vocal demand for reform by elite groups has met determined opposition from Muslims throughout the subcontinent. Partial and hesitant reforms in Pakistan evoked no response in Indian Muslim communities. It has occurred to no one that anthropological investigation, carried out in close liaison with lawyers, might reveal from a sufficient number of typical communities, more or less localised or more or less sophisticated, that the archaic features in Indian Muslim law (as contrasted with the reformed Muslim law of Middle Eastern countries) had a function, unexpectedly vital and continuing which a brash, sledge-hammer reform would turn into yet another source of evasion, corruption, and chaos. The impatience with which Muslim 'intransigence' is treated in the academic world, and the naive assumption by teachers of family law in Asia that Islamic law does not deserve to be protected (subject to some items which Muslim law teachers do not fail to point to as useful for all communities), join the general apathy to reassure the government that real research by skilled persons (as opposed to Town Hall meetings) is not worth paying for.

The same problem of personal and tribal laws is parallel to the problem of a national language, which has also had to be fostered artificially, and surely the anthropologists' oil could have been poured on those troubled waters more often than it has been. Perhaps foreigners and foreign-trained native experts would do better to remember that the histories of developed countries are very different; and that it is foolish to copy them in an untimely unification rather that to treat seriously the rich diversity which still obtains, a diversity from which unknown discoveries may arise and developments emerge.

To conclude: The two skills, of the lawyer and of the anthropologist, can be utilised by a third agency, which will be political or administrative in complexion, such as a Law Commission, to identify the public's complaints against the existing law, to identify their actual practices and needs, and to estimate the probabilities, should any proposed scheme for reform of the law be undertaken. Despite the size of the territories in question, the supply of anthropologists is adequate to meet the need, and it is known that lawyers are superabundant.

This brings me to a caveat. The third agency can work well with the aid of the two skills only if it functions without interference from unseen advisors. Not more than a very limited value can be attributed to India's (and other countries'?) habit of employing expatriates to come, to give olympian advice, and go away. This is at times combined with a few natives' shorter research trips abroad to study with foreign 'experts', the candidates for this honour being selected on the basis of their prestige-rating at home rather than their knowledge of or aptitude for pursuing the subject-matter. Experts in these fields are often mere catalysts; the elements that function remain behind the screen. When the time is ripe for action to be taken the expert's advice, hitherto ignored, is trotted out as the ostensible reason for the programme. The nearer the 'expert' is to understanding the real factors and projecting a realistic programme the less credit he will be given and the less overt notice will be taken of his suggestions.

India, Sri Lanka, and to the best of my knowledge Africa, will do well enough to find out about their own customs and laws, to project them in their own ways, and to reform them by their own instrumentalities. Anthropologists are needed for the factual study of what people actually do and want. These must be men and women who can take up the task in collaboration with lawyers and, more particularly, law-teachers, as understood in the territories in question, and can stay, making a career, or part-career out of it. In this way developing countries can perfect a tool for their own development which the so-called developed countries never invented.

Appendix.

This present volume was in contemplation in 1972-73. Perhaps not by coincidence heart-searchings on the subject of law and development were already afoot. Searching enquiries into the real effectiveness of the United States Law, etc., were accumulating. The devastating, and convincing studies of Marc Galanter[1] on the almost inevitable inequities of a developed legal system, as all common-law territories know it, bring home what was more than suspected in various quarters somewhat earlier. A recent contribution by David M. Trubek and Marc Galanter[2] covers, more fully and elegantly, many of my contentions above. Their theme is the sad state of part-time law-and-development scholars who for too long lent themselves to a naive assistance programme, based upon false hypotheses as to the virtue of changes which American money was attempting to induce in so-called under-developed territories. Now that the widow's cruse runs dry the moral soundness of these programmes is queried aloud. But, I submit, this does not mean that lawyers should not seek the aid of anthropologists (and vice versa) in locally-based research-programmes with much more realistic (and un-patronising) aims in view, such as I have

---

1) 'Why the 'haves' come out ahead: speculations on the limits of legal change', *Law and Society Review* 9/1, Fall 1974, 95-160; 'Afterword: explaining litigation', *ibid.* 9/2, Winter 1975, 347-368.
2) 'Scholars in self-estrangement: some reflections on the crisis in law and development studies in the United States', *Wisconsin Law Review* 1974/1, 1062-1102.

adumbrated. Meanwhile we all need to remember something of which they rightly remind us:

'Legal training provides elaborate categories for remembering and analysing rules but treats other elements of the legal process haphazardly, inducing a learned incapacity to perceive, recall, and analyze the system in actual operation. Legal scholarship concentrates on the work of precisely those levels and areas of the system which the paradigm fits best. Furthermore, the normative element in the paradigm reinforces its descriptive use by labelling each counter-instance as deviant and therefore 'bad','[3]

This is precisely where the anthropologist may come into his own.

3) *Op. cit.*, p. 1082.

Anthropologists probably know more about land tenure in traditional societies than most other social scientists. Yet the decisions taken about traditional land tenure seldom reflect the perspective of an anthropological analysis. Anthropologists can bridge the gap between themselves and those who decide land tenure policies.

My paper on land alienation shows the fairly basic kinds of things that can be done by an anthropologist with legal training to alleviate some of the tensions caused by modern development. I try to illuminate the hiatus between lawyers and anthropologists; each knows little about the work of the other, though there is, as this paper shows, need for a joint contribution.

THE IMPORTANCE OF LEGAL AND ANTHROPOLOGICAL TRAINING

Glynn Cochrane

As an undergraduate at Dublin University I studied modern history and political science. I had originally been admitted as a medical student, and my change to history was greeted with horror by my academic adviser. He caused me of taking the 'easy way out' with those 'soft, liberal arts types'. After I graduated I went to Oxford for postgraduate training. Because I was going into the British Overseas Civil Service, and because by virtue of my position I would be, *ex officio*, a magistrate, I had to take courses and pass exams in law. When I went to the Pacific I had still more law courses and law exams to complete. In the end I knew enough law to pass degree and professional exams in Britain. At the same time I had learned enough anthropology to be able to do fieldwork.

This paper focuses on the kinds of problems I encountered in the Solomons where, as an administrator, I often supervised or negotiated alienation of customary lands. As a result of my anthropological and legal training, I was able to attempt to analyze and resolve some of the resulting difficulties within the context of land policy. Without this legal training, I doubt whether it would have been possible to make any useful contribution. Similarly, what I could do was determined to a large extent by knowledge of administrative resources. My aim was simply to try as far as possible to analyze the traditional system so that transfers could be carried out in a manner that would make them acceptable from the point of view of both legal systems. What this experience does is to illustrate on a small scale the way in which academic training can be translated into actions that help ease some of the stresses and tensions of development.

I received many complaints from traditionalists that would never have arisen had any attempt been made to establish, to the satisfaction of all interested parties, exactly where a piece of land's boundaries were. Parties to an alienation should, if possible, inspect the land together and agree on boundaries. They should then record the agreement. This can be an administrative rather than a purely legal matter. In West Africa, for example, there was apparently a custom of making sure that the agreement was witnessed by some important neutral person held in high esteem by both sides (Mifsud, 1967:26). Unfortunately, many officials believe a survey carried out by a licensed surveyor is all that is required to establish conclusively the physical dimensions of property. Many surveyors do not appreciate that they themselves represent officialdom.

When cadastral surveys were being carried out on Malaita in the Solomons, it was difficult to persuade people to permit the men to set up control points on mountain tops. The surveyors were threatened with physical violence on several occasions. Pagans thought that the surveyors were insensitive to their beliefs, and had no intention of accepting the accuracy of the survey. They suspected that the Government was trying to steal their ground. Subsequently, in areas surveyed with an accuracy that would have been acceptable in Sydney, I found that the only method local people were prepared to accept was to 'walk the spearline' (boundary). It was usually necessary when undertaking alienation in traditional areas to do two surveys, one for officials and one for local people.

It is also important in delineating physical characteristics to find out or know the answers to such questions as: What is the traditionalist position with respect to minerals? If land is alienated, do the mineral rights also pass simultaneously? Traditionalists have sometimes asserted that they retained the mineral rights while purchasers have held that they had bought them. There is among Melanesians great opposition to, and rejection of, any idea that Government owns all mineral rights. Unless more care is taken to reconcile these conflicting ideas, then the investment of mining companies will be in great danger. The experience of the threatened Government geologists surveying on Malaita underlines the necessity for precautionary measures.

Care must also be taken to check carefully other fictions that are ingrained in modern land legislation. These are: Is the boundary between lands divided by a watercourse the centre of the stream? Are walls or fences separating properties divided in the middle, and does each owner have the right of support? Where land is bounded by the sea, is the high water mark the extremity, the low water mark, or what? These things can be important. In North Malaita, I have seen a dispute between two Melanesians, whose land was divided by a stream, when they discovered a geologist in the water taking samples of iron pyrites. They thought he had discovered gold. Disputes arise over the repair of stone walls dividing garden plots and plantation trees. Lands bordering the sea are often thought by traditionalists to include offshore reefs. I once found that an Australian-based company stirred up feeling among traditionalist Solomon Islanders by having strangers catch crayfish on reefs that the islanders felt were theirs.

The message of all this is simple: all the assumptions of modern land law concerning boundaries ought to be carefully checked (see for Fiji, France 1969:146) in an attempt to reach common agreement on what the nature and extent of a piece of land may be. But, despite Government declarations that native customs are to be honored, these things are not systematically done as a matter of course prior to alienation anywhere in the Pacific islands.

This brings me to the second important point, the exact nature of the interest being alienated. It is a universal principle that a man cannot grant to another an interest greater than that which he possesses or is empowered to grant. Such an attempt would be *ultra vires*. Therefore one always needs to try to find out the precise nature of the interest that sellers purport to possess and purchasers purport to receive.

Broadly speaking, I always began alienation proceedings by assuming that traditionalist groups which possessed the ultimate title to land granted two kinds of occupational license in the Solomons: a) a kind of usufructuary title held during the individual tenant's good behavior for life or a term of years; b) a land grant type of title to an individual held during good behavior, though it may often be assigned *inter vivos* or by a tenant's testamentary disposition without prior consent of the group. Alternatively, where ultimate ownership was thought to vest in the ancestors, members of the group could be considered to act as trustees. As such, they also make grants to individuals similar to a) and b).

These I should stress are general outlines. The tenurial customs of each area tend to be unique in some sense. A Nigerian example emphasizes that traditional tenurial systems can often possess unique features: 'The interest of each member of a family in family land is neither strictly usufructuary in the Roman sense, nor is it a tenancy in common or a joint tenancy according to English law. Again it is not proprietory in the sense that it carries such a complete power of disposal as is enjoyed by an English fee simple owner of land; it is equally inaccurate to regard it as merely possessory, for the occupier ordinarily enjoys a degree of freedom of use which a fee simple owner might envy. It is clear that the Nigerian occupier of family land is not a life-tenant of his holding such as is his opposite number in an English settlement, and he would be the first to admit that his interest is not fully hereditary although he would quickly add that his offspring could not be lightly disinherited from his own allotment by the surviving members of his own family. And, to the extent that his interest may come to an end . . . it seems that he holds a kind of fee conditional or even fee determinable, which however, is peculiarly indigenous' (see Jedege, 1970, where this is quoted; Elias, 1951:157; Meek, 1957:76, 77; Lloyd, 1962:79, 80).

Economic trees, such as coconuts and coffee, planted on another's land illustrate an important point in the physical delineation of property. Trees and land are, in the Solomons, separate types of property. With a growth in cash cropping, this traditional custom of a land holder permitting another person to plant trees on his land underwent change. An attempt has frequently been made in recent years by land holders to have the owners of trees pay some money to the man on whose ground they stood. This usually failed. Since the granting of a right to plant trees had been a discretionary privilege, it has been withdrawn by land holders. Therefore, despite assurances by land owners that all trees, economic or otherwise, are theirs, claims should be carefully checked to see how the rights are held and how they may be extinguished.

How, then, do individuals hold land of their lineage in a traditionalist area? The individual tenant's lease is at the pleasure of the lineage. It can, in theory, be cancelled for bad behavior. Individuals hold their ground by virtue of personal status and the rendering of personal service to the group. But failure to act correctly may not result in loss of an individual's land rights in progressive cash cropping areas. There are large numbers of absentee tenants from these places in towns. Sometimes they stay there for years. While it is true that their rights may weaken. I did not see a negative prescriptive claim on grounds of absenteeism made in Native Courts serving these progressive areas.

Where ultimate ownership resides with ancestral spirits, the requirement seems to be that the living adhere to traditional norms and practices known to be favored by the ancestors. While these beliefs persist, it is not possible to alienate these grounds permanently because those making such an attempt would be disposing of something that was not within their prerogative. Such alienations have often caused resentment.

Several times I asked Solomon Islanders in remote areas if anyone claimed lands that appeared to be unoccupied or uncultivated. This kind of question was important where Government intended to establish forest preserves encompassing remote and supposedly vacant lands. But even seemingly vacant areas often contain nut trees, old village sites, and old sacred places. Rarely did anyone go off and claim these grounds. When Solomon Islanders living in the bush are asked if property is possessed they tend to think of the characteristics of ground that is 'owned' by Europeans. Vacant lands in the bush do not have these characteristics, and so often natural reply is that the lands are not held by anyone.

Asking about how property is held is important in the context of alienation since such questions can illuminate many common misunderstandings. Europeans cannot hold their interest in a piece of property in a traditional Melanesian manner (Crocomb, 1968:66). But Melanesians have obviously, in some instances, expected their tenants to behave in a traditional manner like any other usufructuary or life tenant. In North Malaita, Government had leased ground from a group of Melanesians to build a rest house for touring officers. Assuming the trees on the site to be Government property, an agricultural officer began taking fruit from them. This was construed as theft by the tree owners — who were not the same people as the group the Government had its lease agreement with — and bloodshed was only narrowly averted. The nature of the interest that passed to Government as a consequence of leasing had not been clearly identified.

Lease arrangements in the private sector are unusual. Because of difficulties and dangers in trying to achieve arrangement between local people and aliens on this question of leasing, a number of countries were against permanent alienation or leasing to non-locals (see T.P.N.G. 1962-65; B.S.I.P. 1959,

1964; Maimi, 1967:8). There is an easily understandable resentment over what has often happened to leased lands (A. L. Epstein, 1969:137; Wilson, 1969:117).

But where Government lease arrangements are concerned there is usually uncertainty over the amount of rent that should be paid when ground is leased from traditionalist groups. There is even more uncertainty over what should happen to permanent structures and fixtures created on the property during the life of the lease.

It would be impossible, given traditional norms, to achieve any individualistic legal apportionment of rent where group ownership is concerned. The problem was recognized in Kenya: 'Where the land, lease or charge is owned jointly, no proprietory is entitled to any separate share and consequently dispositions may be made only by all the joint proprietors' (Kenya 1963: section 102).

Payment of rent to a small number of individual members of the owning group alters the traditional position significantly. Each member then receives a definite sum of money. Service of tenants had been owed to and enjoyed by the entire community; but payment of rent often ignored the weak, the old, and the very young since they did not receive a share.

What can be done to reduce tensions in Government lease arrangements? If a large number of group members can be collected then something can be done to narrow the gap between our concept of rent and the Melanesian rendering of group service. Here the notion of a trust has much to recommend it. Establishment of a bank or savings account in the name of the group can be useful when the compounding of service for money is inevitable and the social and economic conditions do not suggest that the time is ripe for more fully blown concepts of individualism. When the total is large enough, and when all are agreed, the money can be spent on something that will benefit the entire group. In traditionalist areas such accounts have been used to purchase village radios, a wharf, a new roof for the church. This is not ideal, though it has appeal in that it reduces conflict. For many Solomon Islanders, trusts are more in keeping with the spirit of customary practices with respect to the leasing of lands.

Negotiations for lease or purchase with a group are difficult. There may be a large number of members. Negotiating for land to be used in airfield construction in the Solomons, I frequently met and talked with upwards of 300 people. Obviously, a key problem is getting all those people together. This must be attempted. Such meetings lessen the chance of fraud on the part of a few who might otherwise try to present themselves as absolute owners; they can also serve to avoid later charges of poor faith.

With group-held lands, if a permanent alienation was not to be *ultra vires* from the traditionalist point of view, I usually considered that the following conditions would have to be satisfied: a) all members of the group, or as many as possible, would have to signify consent; b) the group must possess the radical title; c) payment must be made to the group as a whole; d) both sides must acknowledge and confirm that they have the necessary capacity to enter into such a legal relationship and that there is mutual understanding over the nature and meaning of the agreement; e) arrangements for easements and servitudes connected with the property must have been satisfactorily negotiated and settled.

Dealing with a), it needs to be emphasized that by himself an individual of the traditional group owns nothing. When a member dies, this interest can be considered to have been absorbed by the survivors (Cochrane, 1971 (c)). If all members were to die save one infant, then the property would vest in him. Therefore, unless some method were devised to let babies signify their consent, it is in theory at least difficult to make a legal alienation. Any transfer by less than the total number of living members can in theory be regarded as *ultra vires*. Those who act in such a case purport to alienate something that they do not in fact own. But we live in an imperfect world and so, despite this fine point, transfers take place based on consensus and the absence of strong dissent.

Dealing with b), it can be seen that where the radical title is thought to vest in the ancestors, the living have no right to alienate the land (Maini 1967:6; Meek 1957:132). In such instances, the group appears to have a perpetual lease, something known in Roman law as *emphyteusis*. If the group is converted to Christianity, then the problem is obviously less complex.

The stipulations made earlier in discussion of the apportionment of rent are also relevant in the case of c). Individuals can no more alienate a portion of the group lands than they can spend on their own account the proceeds from permanent alienation.

The suggestion made in d) is hard to accomplish. I have often known that all the lineage members had not come forward during the negotiations for permanent alienation. They did not subsequently complain. But there is no knowing what future generations will think of that sale even though every effort was made to explain and to obtain the consent of the widest number of people. It was found useful to allow for a period of one or two years prior to closing the sale. This is usually an adequate amount of time to get word to all interested parties.

Finally e), which usually includes purchase of existing trees that stand on the property or rights of tree cutting, fishing, or hunting. When a decision to purchase outright is taken, it is vital at the earliest opportunity to count and record all trees of value. The existence of sacred places, paths, rights of access and all other easements and servitudes must be noted. There are sound reasons for haste. I have known of some instances where a decision to purchase was widely publicized some two years prior to the announced date for alienation. In that intervening period the ground was planted with thousands of young trees. On another occasion, I discovered people erecting shrines in the centre of a piece of ground to be purchased.

The conflicts briefly dealt with in this paper can, I believe, be found in other areas where there is uneven development. Effective treatment should require that a tenurial system should have good fit with local socio-economic conditions and that legislation should be flexible in the case of traditionalist groups. It should be possible for legal anthropologists to analyze customary forms of tenure and to continue analysis with the object of appreciating the salient features of a living body of law. These findings could be used to reduce conflict between legal systems that can imperil economic and social development and can also contribute significantly to hostility between ethnic groups. The administrative requirements of such a course are not excessive. But if anthropological insights are to be useful in such a context, then anthropologists interested in land tenure must have some basic training in law.

Bibliography

Abensour, E. S. (1966), *Principles of Land Tenure Legislation.* Rome.

Allan, C. H. (1957), *Customary Land Tenure in the British Solomon Islands Protectorate.* London.

Brookfield, H. C. and P. Brown (1963), *Struggle for Land.* Melbourne.

British Solomon Islands, Protectorate Government.
(1959) *Lands and Titles Ordinance.*
(1964) *Lands and Titles (Amendment) Ordinance.*

Cochrane, G.
(1970) (b) *Big Men and Cargo Cults.* Oxford.
(1971) (a) *Development Anthropology.* New York.
(1971) (b) 'Use of the Concept of Corporateness: A Choice Between Colloquialism or Distortion', *American Anthropologist*, Vol.5.
(1971) (c) 'Juristic Persons, Group and Individual Land Tenure: A Rejoinder to Goodenough', *American Anthropologist*, Vol.5.

Crocomb, R.G. (1964), *Land Tenure in the Cook Islands.* Melbourne.
(1968), *Improving Land Tenure.* Noumea.

Dowson, E. and V. L. O. Sheppard (1956), *Land Registration.* (2nd ed.). London.

Dyal, E., C. Elliott (1966), *Land Tenure.* Geneva.

East African Royal Commission (1955), *Report.* London.

Elias, T. O. (1951), *Nigerian Land Law and Custom.* London.

Epstein, A. L. (1939), *Matupit, Land, Politics and Change Among the Tolai of New Britain.* Berkeley.

66

France, P. (1969), *The Charter of the Land.* Melbourne.

Government of Andhra Pradesh (1965), *The Land Acquisition Manual.*

Hailey, Lord (1949), Introduction to C. K. Meek, *Land Law and Custom in the Colonies.* London.

Jegede, M. I. (1970), 'Nature and Extent of Family Member's Rights and Interests in Family Land in Nigeria', *East African Law Review,* Vol. 33:229-255.

Kenya Government (1963), *Registered Lands Ordinance.*

Lawrence, P. (1955), *Land Tenure Among the Garia.* Canberra: Australian National University Social Science Monographs, No. 4.

Lloyd, P. C. (1955), *Yoruba Land Law.* London.

Maimi, K. M. (1967), *Land Law in East Africa.* Nairobi.

Mair, L. (1931), 'Native Land Tenure in East Africa', *Africa,* Vol. 4:314-329.
   (1936), *Native Politics in Africa.* London.

Meek, C. K. (1949), *Land Law and Custom in the Colonies.* London.
        (1967), *Land Tenure and Land Administration in Nigeria and the Cameroons.* London.

Mifsud, F. M. (1967), *Customary Land Law in Africa.* Rome.

Nash, P. G. (1968), 'Some Problems of Administering Law in the Territory of Papua and New Guinea', *The Comparative and International Law Journal of South Africa,* Vol. 11, no. 1:208-247.

Okoro, K. (1966), *The Customary Laws of Succession in Eastern Nigeria.* London.

Parsons, K. H., R. H. Penn and P. M. Raup (eds.) (1956), *Land Tenure, Proceedings of the International Congress on World Land Tenure and Related Problems.* Madison.

Pitt, D. (1970), *Tradition and Economic Progress in Samoa.* Oxford.

Sutherland, I. L. G. (1935), *Maori Situation.* Wellington.

Territory of Papua and New Guinea (1962-65), *Land Ordinance.*
   (1963) (a), *Land Tenure (Conversion) Ordinance.*
   (1963) (b), *Native Customs (Recognition) Ordinance.*

Western Pacific High Commission (1964), *Western Pacific High Commission (Courts) Order in Council.* London.

Wilson, M. (1961), *Reaction to Conquest.* (2nd ed.). London.

How difficult is it for graduates of schools of anthropology to settle in to jobs in a nonacademic environment? How well do they think they were prepared for such careers?

Douglas Rider's paper is based on his experience in Alaska. Rider stresses the importance and value of really understanding education, acquiring administrative skills, and a career in the management of change. He feels more should be done to prepare students in graduate schools for such careers. Rider also makes the point that there is a great deal that anthropologists can do in the industrialized countries.

PREPARING FOR TEACHER TRAINING IN THE ALASKAN 'BUSH'

C. Douglas Rider

I now wish that I had had a more interdisciplinary form of training, one that included some exposure to public administration. My training was in anthropology, though I spent some time in educational research. My 'problem' was to use the tools of an anthropologist to solve educational problems for culturally unique people in Alaska.[1] I was trained to operate alone, but I found I had to work as member of a team.

Not all development anthropologists will achieve positions with great power and influence. Students need to be psychologically prepared for this kind of situation. I feel that the 'kind' of individual required will be one whose reward system functions on inner satisfaction, i.e., a job well done rather than his number of publications or his contributions to the professional literature. Graduate students in anthropology are trained as if they were going to become famous anthropologists. More should be done to prepare anthropologists to work in more mundane, anonymous roles.

The intellectual foundations for interdisciplinary training in educational anthropology are not yet firm enough. Often, the anthropological researcher does not focus on educational issues sufficiently to allow educational administrators to use his report in a comparative manner. Several recent monographs have struggled with educational concerns. But I felt that the authors went to the field and did their fieldwork in a traditional fashion, focusing on social structure, economic patterns of kinship. Then, *ex post facto*, the ethnographer returned to his field notes to dredge out what he could on education, often confounding concepts, i.e., acculturation, enculturation, socialization, education and schooling.

My Experience in Alaska

In June 1971 I became the university coordinator for the Alaska Rural Teacher Training Corps (hereafter to be called ARTTC). The institutional participants are Alaska Methodist University, the University of Alaska (Fairbanks), and the Alaska State-Operated School System. My duties included working with the university staff and faculty to enable them to understand the educational objectives of the ARTTC program. I was to provide leadership in developing a more detailed instructional program for the ARTTC students than had to that time been developed. I was to facilitate communications between my university (Alaska Methodist) and the other participants in ARTTC. I was to assure that participating staff members were kept informed about the progress of the program. Finally, it was my duty to transmit information and coursework to the villages where the students were in training.

The ARTTC program is a four-year undergraduate program leading to an undergraduate degree in education and an Alaskan teaching credential. The students at the time I entered the program numbered about 55. The majority of the students were Alaska Indian and Eskimo; however, there were a number of non-Natives recruited at the upper-division level (junior and senior) because we could not find a sufficient number of Alaska Natives with two years of college. The administration and staff were all non-Native. The 'staff' consisted of a director, who is part of the Alaska State-Operated School System. His training and previous experience had been in a field other than education. The director's staff consisted of eleven team leaders and a secretary. Team leaders were supposed to have taught in the Bush for several years and possess a master's degree. The program brought in close contact the following cultural groups: Western, Eskimo, Athabascan, Tsimshian, Tlingit, Haida and Aleut. The geographical scope of the program was immense. Gaylen Searles, a team leader who is now the school principal at Point Hope, attended a regional meeting of Teacher Corps programs. During the meeting one of the participants from a large West Coast city lamented that it often took him an hour to drive to monitor one of his teams. But if often took us three to four hours to fly between our sites, and there was not one that we could drive to except on snowmachine or dogsled.

The problem was to capitalize on what anthropologists knew of traditional informal methods of culture transmission and apply this to instruction within the context of the ARTTC program. If students worked in small groups in the village we felt that they would be closer to the method of informal education used by Native parents to socialize their children. The field-based focus of ARTTC was our vehicle for accomplishing this characteristic of our teacher training program. The students spend their time in the village (September through June) studying the various taped lessons and the coursework sent through the mail. We liked to distinguish the coursework from correspondence work because the academic material was prepared specially (in most cases) for our students. We were aware of various students' strengths and weaknesses and we attempted to interject this knowledge into their academic work. Our first application in the whole development process, then, was to individualize instruction while maintaining small work groups in the villages. We wanted to make a fact out of the educational cliché of 'take your students where they are'.

A number of our students had gone only as far as the fifth and sixth grades in elementary school while others were honor graduates from Indian (BIA) high schools. Therefore, the small groups in the villages were often composed of individuals with a varying commitment to the community. So, while some students transmitted educational knowledge, strength and confidence to others in the group, they received knowledge, strength and confidence in the village culture and community by contact with individuals exhibiting the normative behavior of the community.

It was the purpose of the university coordinator and the development specialist to encourage the instructors to build their courses upon a different premise. Indeed, we urged the professor to look for skills and abilities in our students that often didn't receive academic credit. We attempted to point out cultural differences and similarities that could affect instruction. We espoused education as a cultural process rather than cultural content.

Our effort centered on identifying universal processes of education and encouraging the Indian and Eskimo student to supply their own content. Studying in the village allowed much more of the 'cultural content' adaption. We were aware that many of our students compared with urban students lacked a great deal of exposure to content based on western ideas and beliefs. We attempted to convey to the university instructor that western ideas and beliefs, usually the foundations of his or her course, were not singularly important to the rural person who wanted to become a 'bush' teacher. It was our hope that the student and professor would draw on the cultural content of the student for the application of the principles the teacher was attempting to convey.

The factors that militated against the success of changing teacher training were the teachers that our students worked with, the other teacher trainers at our institutions, and various teacher certification boards. When one of the participating universities after long deliberation decided to adopt a cross-cultural approach to teacher training, many long months of planning paid us dividends. It is most difficult to attribute change to any single person or any single contribution from a social science. Success depended on ability to move between the disciplines of education and anthropology, between local client groups and between large bureaucratic institutions in order to bring problems to satisfactory solutions.

I found it was necessary to take the expressed needs of the ARTTC students and modify them to the physical situation of a university campus designed for single students. The academic coursework, though important, was secondary to the social aspects that the summer could afford. The educational benefits of bringing together in one place people from all the Alaskan Native cultures could be tremendous, but so could the liabilities if the summer was improperly handled. The three months that the students are not in the 'Bush' they are on the campus of one of the participating universities. The ARTTC students are often apprehensive about the nature of urban and campus life and the unique opportunity it may provide. The students live in the 'Bush' because it is home, and they do not like to be separated from their families. In fact, one of the virtues of the ARTTC approach (the field-centered approach) to teacher training is that the student does not have to leave home for the major part of his academic training.

Many Alaska Natives have spent up to twelve years away from home before they graduate from high school. A common reminder of this is the 'hiatus of the young' ritual at the end of every summer when many Native high school students board the 'Wein plane' to return to schools that may be as far as 3,000 miles away from the village. Any parent can imagine the unpleasantness of sending his child from San Francisco to Chicago or New York to attend high school. Urban educators often talk about the harm of bussing. I am sure the harm to the Alaska family of 'airplaning' is obvious. Therefore, in our summer planning we make every effort to keep the family unit intact.

In cases where unwanted family separation did occur, we usually experienced personal problems with the student. For example, an Eskimo student arrived on campus with his new bride. It wasn't long before she asked to return to her mother in southwestern Alaska. In a very short time after his wife's departure the young man was in an acute state of melancholia. We felt that it was necessary to break the rules to allow the young man to return to his village before the end of the term. His performance had taken such a serious turn for the worse that any effort to keep him would have jeopardized his opportunity for remaining eligible for college. He has subsequently returned to the ARTTC program and his performance is quite satisfactory.

In making housing arrangements for the incoming ARTTC students we worked hard to get the housing authorities to agree to putting a man, wife, their three children, and wife's sister in a dormitory room designed for two single college students. The housing authorities were concerned about the possible health problems of such an arrangement. Our dilemma was that we saw each point of view: the student does not want to leave his family at home; the housing authorities are responsible for the well-being of the student population. Our solution was to convince the housing people that the student lived in an even smaller area in the village and frequently they had no running water or flush toilets. This meant that despite the crowded conditions on-campus they would have a better opportunity to practice a greater degree of health care. We then displayed several pictures of housing conditions from our visits to the 'Bush', and we were granted our request.

One of our greatest problems was making sure the young children of the students were adequately looked after so that the students themselves had time for classes and study. Whether it was a matter of cultural difference or individual preference, many of the parents were quite casual about the behavior of their children. In the village the children are acquainted with the boundaries of proper behavior; however, in town with so many unfamiliar rules and structures it was a constant battle to keep them from harming each other or themselves. This often gave the casual onlooker the impression that Native parents do not prac-tice any form of discipline. The truth of the matter is that the Native American parents have inculcated their children with behavior that is appropriate for the village, not for the urban environment.

The Lessons of Experience

I was an applied anthropologist working in an educational setting. I was doing much more than applying an anthropological perspective. Educational research-ers are well acquainted with survey methods. The long-term field study that is the trademark of the anthropologist is not accepted — if not acceptable to them on methodological grounds, then certainly on financial grounds. Research so emphasized in my anthropological training seems to be a luxury rather than a tool and cannot be tolerated by many program budgets. We always seemed to be under pressure to write this proposal, submit that concept, or answer the questions of some evaluation team.

I was constantly asked questions about the Native cultures and the Native feelings, but rarely was I seen as an important source of information on educa-tion in general. Usually my comments on educational practices and procedures were accepted only if they concerned problems directly related to the Native.

An anthropologist, I was taught, doesn't play politics; he or she usually observes them being played. In administration this could lead to a very high mortality rate. 'Politics' seem to be a way of life for the administrator that must be learned and mastered for survival. The task, then, was for me to gain credibility in the system within which I performed my role. It was not enough to be considered the 'Native expert'. My anthropological training had improper-ly prepared me for the role I was playing, and this did curtail my usefulness to the bureaucracy. I did not have the luxury of saying that I could not or would not decide on a direction. My point of view was not as objective as it should have been. Nowhere in my training, my teaching, or my professional work has anyone been able to convince me that there is only one right way or best way either 'anthropological' or 'educational' to accomplish a task.

I experienced conflict between educational and anthropological values. A teacher is charged with acting as a prime transmitter of change with respect to school children. The anthropologist who balks at being involved in change and acting as a change agent should reflect on the fact that when a child walks into a classroom our society dictates that he experience some form of social change. In fact, many anthropologists who themselves advocate a humanistic perspective and endeavor to impart a feeling for cultural relativism in their own classroom teaching often castigate lower-grade teachers for attempting to impart values. Training in anthropology teaches you that there are many sets of values and beliefs, but not that one set is better than another, just more or less appropriate given the total cultural context. An educationalist must inculcate specific values. Can anthropologists even be teachers? This is the kind of human problem that interdisciplinary work presents.

I have had colleagues who questioned my professional affiliation with a program directed toward changing the status of Native Americans. They felt that 'we' anthropologists should leave them to their own devices. My reply, which is less than profound, was always that the Native people surely deserved the opportunity to make decisions about their future; by becoming school teachers they would influence the direction their culture would take by transmitting their values and desires to their own children. In professional education or schooling, a person performing as an administrator must often make value judgments.

There is a basic conflict in what sorts of activities and problems intrigue the student and encourage him to take on a major in anthropology and those kinds of interests that encourage a person to pursue an administrative career. How does an anthropologist do some good? How does he know he has the requisite skills? How does he know what the intellectual and social reward system will be? All these things are important and require interdisciplinary training. For instance, educational administrators often receive premium pay. Salary is not usually the reason why one becomes an anthropologist. The position must provide some other rewards than just remuneration. This is not to say that the professional administrator functions purely on a high financial reward schedule. Rather, I think it is important to suggest that many administrators function well in their role because it provides a challenge to their ability to organize and to handle people.

What an administrator thrives on is usually anathema to the person interested in the exotic and longing for the adventure of contact with alien cultures rather than hassling with bureaucratic red tape. As I embarked on my career in educational administration, my problem revolved around how to do anthropology in such a way as to bring its perspective to bear on educational planning and problem-solving. In my experience the rural Alaskan did not distinguish between the bureaucrat and the anthropologist. The nature of development work as I see it, for people with any background and interests, is a long-term commitment to working for change in positions demanding the need to participate in decision making. In view of my experience I advocate involvement.

74

Note.

1) George Spindler as late as 1965 lamented that there cannot be more than a dozen anthropologists actively working on educational process in our own society, and he could see no encouraging signs that there would be many more than this in the immediate future. There are studies that, though not strictly anthropological, contribute toward an understanding of the type of problems that I am addressing. In African education significant contributions are: Phillip J. Foster, *Education and Society in Ghana*, 1965; Margaret Read, *Education and Social Change in Tropical Areas*, 1955; Millie Almy, Joel Davitz, and Mary White, *Studying School Children in Uganda*, 1970. For those readers with an interest in Latin America, Malvina R. McNeill, *Guidelines to Problems of Education in Brazil*, 1970.

What can be done to create new employment opportunities for suitably trained anthropologists? Making the writing of anthropologists more available to potential employers is, of course, one way. Another useful approach would be actually to demonstrate how anthropology could relate to institutional problems and performance. Following this research one could assess overall institutional needs, in order to make employment recommendations. This paper gives details of such a strategy carried out at the World Bank.

ANTHROPOLOGY AT THE WORLD BANK

Glynn Cochrane

There is a need to show how public administration and anthropology can use-fully combine. Over fifty years ago, Bronislaw Malinowski, one of the intel-lectual progenitors of modern anthropology, undertook an anthropological analysis of the accumulation and distribution of a few hundred dollars of shell wealth in the remote Trobriand Islands group of the Western Pacific. His pur-pose was to explain to the 'developed' world that Trobriand Islanders were 'primitive' only insofar as their technology was concerned, there being nothing rudimentary about their mental processes. Using many of the same techniques and methods as Malinowski, a colleague and I recently undertook an analysis of some of the activities that surround the accumulation and distribution of several billions of dollars in the World Bank in downtown Washington, D.C.; our purpose was to explain to staff members of an international banking com-munity the worthwhile nature of an anthropologist's mental processes.[1]

Public administration, like anthropology, usually involves mapping out the nature and types of social relationship in an organization. Asking questions about the manner of their arrangement yields an appreciation of organizational structure; finding the reasons for change or maintenance in those relationships can yield an account of the styles of beliefs and values which may be unique to that institution.[2] The kind of analysis practiced by public administration is not a particularly obscure discipline. As a rather gross simplification one might say that, as in the case of anthropology, the virtue lies in being able to ask the right questions of the right people. The aim is to account for and ex-plain organizational behavior which, though perfectly rational when viewed against the underlying and interlocking system of beliefs and values of a particular institution, may be very different from what we would expect. It is quite feasible to wed anthropological techniques to the skills and concerns of public administration.

---

1) The World Bank is now dispersing in loan funds around $3 billion dollars annually. For a detailed report of activities see the World Bank's Annual Reports.
2) See for example, C. Argyris, *Organization and Innovation* (1965), *Some Causes of Organizational Ineffectiveness Within the Department of State* Center for International Systems Research Occasional Paper No. 2); M.E.Dimock et al., *Public Administration*, 1960.

A knowledge of public administration can help because anthropology, of course, has been university-based, and this academic orientation has meant that anthropologists have not as yet as a class had sufficient opportunity to develop and accumulate the kind of institutional experience which would help place their contribution into the integrated framework of policies and practices that characterize the work of institutions in charge of modern development. Part of the problem has been the training in modern schools of anthropology which pays insufficient attention to development work; the counterpart has been a lack of institutional lead in the sense of large public enterprises providing incentives through creation of a demand for adequately trained anthropologists.

In early 1970 the World Bank presented an opportunity to test the belief that adequately trained development anthropologists had something useful to contribute. The Bank was then moving from a pattern of lending in the fields of power, communications, etc., where the risk factor was perhaps reasonably calculable, to increased lending for agriculture, population, and education where behavioral assessments, from an anthropological view, might be both more important and more difficult to make.[3] Anthropology, in view of its accumulation of experience and data on poor communities all over the world, would, it was hoped, be well equipped to assist in the systematic treatment of social issues — the problems of jobs, income distribution, and poor people.[4]

It seemed desirable that the utility of anthropology should be demonstrated to the satisfaction of staff members within the context of existing operations, that the potential work load should be estimated, and that recommendations should then be made to the Bank. An overview of the institution's work would be crucial to this endeavor. Equally crucial would be the demonstration — *doing* anthropology instead of writing about it — because as time passed there was no evidence to show that anthropology and the Bank would establish an effective relationship if things continued as they were.[5] The Bank's operations were not well known to anthropologists: the writing of anthropologists was not getting through to very busy staff members, and the imperatives of development were not getting through to anthropologists.

I submitted to the Bank a research proposal detailing what I wanted to do,

3) See Warren C. Baum, 'The Project Cycle' *Finance and Development*, Vol. 7, No. 2, June 1970; John A. King, *Economic Development Projects and Their Appraisal*, Johns Hopkins Press, 1967; Bernard Chadenet and John A. King, 'What is a World Bank Project?', *Finance and Development*, September 1972.
4) See *Effective Aid*, a discussion published by the Overseas Development Institute, London, 1967, pp. 19-21.
5) Robert F. Meagher, 'The World Bank and Non-Economic Aspects of Development: Some Questions Posed', A.I.D., Research Paper, 1970, Washington D.C.

and this work plan, which called for a fifteen-month analysis of the Bank's project operations to see where anthropology might be useful and what methods could be employed to make this contribution available, was approved. Raymond Noronna, who had just completed his doctorate at Syracuse, then volunteered his assistance.

I had been trained as an administrator and had served for six years in the British Overseas and diplomatic services. I firmly believed in the importance of an administrative training for students in anthropology. After all, of the social and natural sciences involved in large-scale organizational life today, by far the most influential is administrative science, as some refer to it.

A first requirement when research commenced at the Bank on June 1, 1972, was to learn as much as possible about how the institution actually functioned. It was necessary to learn how one would operate as a staff member before one could attempt to visualize how an anthropological staff member might operate. It was necessary to know how problems were approached, how they were tackled, what the constraints were, what the time frame was, and what kinds of people staff members were. In this way, the Bank could be understood as a system containing a series of well-defined roles, a hierarchical series of levels of authority, a distinct set of values on how things should be done, and a very heavy work program. It was clearly important to assess the willingness of staff members to innovate by using anthropology. What would encourage them to do so, and what might discourage them? Did incentives and disincentives vary with different geographical areas and different types of projects? What was to be learned from recent experience with other innovations? How accurate and realistic were staff members' perceptions of what anthropologists could do? [6]

Answers to such wide-ranging questions were not easy to obtain, and the pursuit involved talking to several hundred staff members. There were some five hundred Bank projects in over eighty countries that might have been looked at, though in practice it was clearly impossible to consider so many. Instead it was decided to draw up a sample of projects from all sectors, e.g., education, agriculture, health, etc. The objective was to analyze projects which were representative of a type of problem commonly experienced or of a particular sector. The results would, we hoped, show that the discipline really needed to be considered a normal and necessary part of project work. It is obvious that all projects affect social relationships in terms of the acquisition and distribution of power, wealth, and status in the societies in which they are located.

It is also now commonplace, though useful, to remark that many people

6) Escott Reid, *The Future of the World Bank*, I.B.R.D., Washington, 1965.

believe that usual methods of evaluation for development involving Gross National Product and percapita growth have not proved entirely adequate. There has been an obvious need to increase the range of quantifiable measures. These new variables to be considered include availability and quality of health services, nutrition levels, housing, clean water, electric power, and sewage facilities. They must obviously be seen as something more than social overhead capital. They can be regarded as necessary though not sufficient variables.

It is, of course, true that people in lesser developed countries will want some of the benefits of modernization, but, inevitably, they will wish to enjoy those benefits in a societal framework and within a traditional culture and rhythm of life. It is one of the tasks of the anthropologist interested in development to find out what that framework is: the beliefs, values, and attitudes that generate structural alignments in the society, the potentialities for change, and what harm may come from the change.

A development project might be a financial success and yet fail to meet social equity of social development goals. How can these social issues be avoided in situations where governments help a small number of farmers to increase their incomes through provision of low-cost finance while those on the edge of the project pay usurious rates for their capital? Anthropology can often help in such cases by working on the local subjective image of poverty and so establishing what those people would be prepared to accept as reasonable. This kind of information can illuminate the problem of distribution; many economists' data seem on the other hand to be about income averaging. There is no 'scientific' way to achieve the best distribution of benefits. All one can, and should, do is take off the rough edges. This of course must be a matter for collaboration because it is fully appreciated that the Bank is dealing with sovereign governments. In many cases these governments may have little enthusiasm for tackling what outsiders consider to be important social issues.

A 'problem' project in development work is usually considered to be one that has failed to live up to standards deemed necessary if fiscal calculations and their various administrative, organizational or institutional arrangements encompassing the project cycle are to be met. Problems are, from the anthropological point of view, often somewhat strangely attributed to broad and culturally meaningless categories seldom anchored by empirical material. An 'administrative' or 'organizational' problem in one culture may have no parallel in another culture. For example, there is not a single agricultural scheme in the world whose failure could not be broadly attributed to one of the criteria used in the project cycle, e.g., 'organizational', 'managerial'. But how far can such a labeling process take us in determining exactly why a project encountered problems? It is necessary to know why *this* project in *this* society has problems or is likely to have problems at *this* time. This is where an anthropologist can frequently help.

Development agencies operate under considerable constraints which are occasioned by an alarming increase in the volume of demands for assistance in recent years. There is, as the *Pearson Report* pointed out, the continuing need to guard the reputation of development agencies in their home countries. The *Pearson Report* did not accept the fact that anthropologists might be useful in development work. Unfortunately, the *Pearson Report* was sadly ill informed about the capability of the noneconomic social sciences.

It is not surprising that when explanation is attempted for projects which have problems from the human point of view one sometimes hears that 'models do not show', or that certain statistics are not adequate. But many of these post-mortems might have been avoided had there been contact with people at the village level at initial stages of the project.[8] Anthropologists cannot, when a project is at or near completion of the project cycle stage, produce data that would have been produced had an anthropologist with the appropriate area facility and experience been associated with the project from the identification stage. This is why participation at the identification stage is often necessary to prove the benefit and utility of the approach. But it is possible to monitor a project in retrospect from two points of view.

First comes an examination of the premises on which the project rested to see if they were socially feasible from the point of view of those who had to do the work. What were the possible effects of change? This question does require professional knowledge, since the unanticipated consequences of social change form an extremely complex and difficult field of study. Based on this one could decide if it would have been desirable to engage an anthropologist as a consultant. Then one could determine what he or she should have been asked to look at.

Second, anthropologists can look at the project in terms of wider objectives. Did it conform to what people in *that* society considered reasonable? What kinds of mechanism were there in that society for diffusion of the kinds of innovation represented by the project? Could anthropological knowledge help ensure that the project had a demonstration effect? Which groups would benefit at the expense of what other groups? In this way one could even in retrospect get a grip on intangibles and, at the same time, pay some attention to social issues.

Would it not be prudent, we suggested to the Bank, in dealing with projects

7) *Partners in Development. Report of the Commission on International Development.* Chairman: Lester B. Pearson. Commissioners: Sir Edward Boyle, Robert de Oliveira Campis, C. Douglas Dillon, Wilfred Gruth, W. Arthur Lewis, Robert E. Marjolin, Saburo Okita. New York, 1969, p. 203.
8) See, for example, J. Price-Gittinger, *The Economic Analysis of Agricultural Projects.* Johns Hopkins Press, 1972.

81

where there is a substantial human element, to begin by assuming that local ₆ reaction would be special and unique until evidence is adduced to the contrary? The present tendency is to assume that if means are provided, then people in different cultures will react in what Euro-Americans consider would be a 'rational' manner. This has not always happened. Yet information is not difficult to obtain.

An institution with global responsibilities may need its staff to have an overview, and a geographical and cultural flexibility, that would make it difficult for anthropologists to operate in terms of their real supposed strength, community knowledge. But it is possible to envisage a system where a permanent cadre of anthropologists based in regions would be able to deal with policy matters, the initial monitoring of projects, and the selection and briefing of specialist consultants when required. It cannot be assumed that the pool of manpower skills developed by development agencies in the past is now sufficient to deal adequately with very poor people.

A second reason lies in the need to provide leadership in dealing with social development issues. Often this leadership is easy to see in research efforts where anthropological insights are frequently involved. But there is usually no clear relationship between the resources devoted by development agencies to research and the resources devoted to their own manpower development. Consequently there is no adequate assurance that the results of research can be applied on the ground in a meaningful way.

A third reason is the matter of public relations. It would make little sense to declare the problems of poor people to be very important and then to have a staffing pattern which excluded or ignored the utility of disciplines that had been dealing with such people in other cultures for over half a century.

A good case for permanent appointment of anthropologists in development agencies can be made, and only by working in a community of staff members that go to make up a development institution can anthropologists provide their best input — a view based on the classic procedures of Malinowski, who felt, half a century ago, that the only way to get his point across was to go and work in the Trobriands. Malinowski's work became the model and inspiration for many similar studies, and it is to be hoped that, on a much more modest level, the approach to anthropology as policy, worked out at the Bank, will stimulate interest in similar studies being carried out at other institutions with bilateral and multilateral responsibilities.[9]

The strategy employed in this study was to learn about banking operations, to apply anthropology to those operations, and to convince staff members that

9) A similar research strategy carried out for the U.S. Agency for International Development in 1973-74 has already resulted in that agency's advertising for the services of a number of anthropologists.

our work was not unique, rather that it represented a standard which was common to anthropology. We worked as a team and instead of wishing to show the value of our own individual approach, we wanted the Bank to accept that there were hundreds of anthropologists like us. When we went to the Bank there was not a single anthropologist staff member. When we left it was agreed that we had made our point. Anthropology became more important. A commitment to hire anthropologists was made and it was accepted that anthropologists should be hired as staff members for the Bank's 'Young Professional' training program.

CONCLUSION

_____

In one sense at least anthropology has never been very democratic: anthropologists choose their community to study; communities do not normally commission an anthropologist of their choice. In the early decades of this century people became anthropologists or studied anthropology because they were personally attracted to the kinds of things that anthropologists did. The discipline was self-contained, anthropologists produced and pretty much entirely consumed their own product. Anthropologists worked in very remote areas where other social scientists didn't seem to want to go, and they addressed themselves to questions that other social scientists didn't seem to want to ask. But as time has passed, anthropologists have begun to run out of very remote areas; more and more people have asked the kinds of questions that originally were of interest only to anthropologists. While broad descriptive ethnographic monographs have continued to have utility, detailed empirical analysis of specific aspects of social life such as agricultural production functions or population control functions have had to draw on the knowledge of other disciplines and professions that specialize in such subject matter. But it is disturbing to see how many introductory works do not deal with the problems for which the Third World has requested assistance.

Currently, in a world troubled by overpopulation, hunger, and disease, there is a need for anthropology to address problems that laymen and representatives from other disciplines take to be important. These same people are becoming consumers of anthropological work and as such they are likely to have a quite profound effect on the development of anthropology in the future. Anthropology urgently needs to reform the way the discipline is taught in order to become less academically oriented and more service oriented.

Anthropology is now being judged by non-anthropologists. Psychologists, economists, and, to an increasing extent, sociologists, have long had to undergo the sobering experience of having their pronouncements gauged against reality, current events, and the experience of people in industrialized nations. But quite a number of anthropological statements have, for many years, had a 'Would You Believe It?' quality because readers in industrialized nations did not have any basis for critical evaluation. But now those who were written about are commenting; political developments have occurred; new problems and perspectives demand attention.

It is one of the strengths of an interdisciplinary approach that it does not require one always to employ the same kinds of methods and theories. There is choice. One of the drawbacks to the argument that occupied economic anthropology for so long, and which centered on the applicability of what economists had done in industrialized countries to the circumstances of 'primitive' societies, was that it tended to imply an 'either/or' decision. One believed, the rather tedious and long-drawn-out debate seemed to suggest, either in the concepts and methods of anthropology or in those of economics when dealing with the production and consumption of goods and services in traditional societies. But there need be no such choice. The posed choice of deductivism *or* inductivism is as false as being an advocate of 'hard' *or* 'soft' data. There is no requirement for the theories and methods of one discipline totally to displace the theories and methods of another discipline. Each will, on occasion, have its use and its own distinctive contribution to make within an interdisciplinary framework.

What is required, and what makes a piece of work interdisciplinary? If engaged on a problem concerning subsistence agriculture an interdisciplinary anthropologist would not take as the sole authority anthropologist 'A's' work simply because he or she had published widely in that field. He or she would need to understand what agricultural science had to say and then would relate this to "A's" work. If working on a problem in economics, one would try to grasp the contributions of development economists as well as economic anthropologists. The result should be an advance for both disciplines. Raymond Firth's symposium, *Themes in Economic Anthropology*, and Max Gluckman's, *The Ideas in Barotse Jurisprudence* are excellent examples. Firth was trained as an economist, Gluckman as a lawyer. The nature of the problem addressed should determine which methods and theories should be used rather than having such decisions based on narrow disciplinary chauvinism.

The performance of scholarly specialist functions will of course continue to play a vital role in the maintenance of a healthy, progressive, alert, and incisive anthropology. But effective anthropology is more and more going to be recognized as the kind that prepares students for non-academic jobs, gets them those jobs, and then ensures that anthropology continues to help raise the level of job performance. Effective anthropology will not depend so much on publication and acceptance of the worthiness of one's statements by fellow academicians, but on getting a job done in a way that earns the approval of other social scientists. It will be the kind of anthropology that does something useful for the kinds of community where anthropologists have worked.

What do the papers in this book indicate? What should be done? Most of today's interdisciplinary anthropologists have been self-taught. On their own, often against the wishes or inclinations of their teachers, they decided that in order to prepare for the kind of work that they wanted to do they would have to have training in several fields. This kind of experience is still valid today. Many students will have to stitch together their own program from the course offerings of their university in order to prepare for their own careers.

But much more is required than individual efforts. The first priority should be to create career employment opportunities. The associations of anthropologists have a valuable role to play in such work. Foundations and other institutions can help by financing research designed to promote the use of anthropology. Demand must be stimulated before able men and women will be prepared to invest a great deal of money training for a non-existent job.

If the necessary institutional demand can be created, then special programs will have to be instituted for development anthropologists. These programs will have to be based on the kinds of suggestions made by the papers in this book. The economic anthropologists, for example, will have training in economics, and the legal anthropologists will have training in law. The norms and values associated with such training will be professional rather than academic. Graduates will be trained to operate as team members and will be given training in public administration. If these things do not soon take place then development anthropology will probably disappear as more and more of the things that anthropologists have traditionally done are undertaken by other social sciences.